Preface

Welcome to Discrete Mathematics: Theory, Problems, and Solutions, a comprehensive resource designed to enhance your understanding of this fundamental area of mathematics. This book is specifically tailored for students, educators, and enthusiasts seeking to deepen their grasp of discrete mathematics through the lens of unsolved and challenging questions.

This book seeks to bridge that gap. By presenting a collection of IGNOU-MCS 212 PREVIOUSLY UNSOLVED QUESTION PAPERS(MCA-NEW), we provide a unique opportunity to engage with the material in a new and dynamic way. Each question is carefully selected to challenge and provoke thought, encouraging a deeper exploration of the subject matter.

Our goal is not only to present problems but to foster a deeper appreciation for the beauty and utility of discrete mathematics. We hope that by working through these questions, you will develop a stronger intuition for the subject and acquire problem-solving skills that will serve you well in both academic and professional contexts.

We extend our heartfelt gratitude to the numerous educators and students who have contributed to the evolution of this book. Their insights and feedback have been invaluable in shaping its content. We also acknowledge the efforts of the authors and researchers whose work has inspired the selection of these problems.

As you embark on this journey through the pages of Discrete Mathematics: Theory, Problems, and Solutions, we encourage you to approach each problem with curiosity and determination. Embrace the challenge, and allow the process of solving these questions to deepen your understanding and appreciation of discrete mathematics.

May this book serve as a valuable tool in your educational endeavors and inspire a lifelong interest in the fascinating world of discrete mathematics.

AF518974

Table of Contents

Master Of Computer Applications (MCA)
Chapter 1: Term-End Examination, December 2021
MCS-212: Discrete Mathematics

Time: 3 Hours
Maximum Marks: 100
Note: Question No. 1 is compulsory and carries 40 marks.
Attempt any three questions from the rest four questions (Question Nos. 2 to 5).

1. (a) Make the truth table for: **5**
   (i) $p \rightarrow q \wedge \sim r$
   (ii) $(p \oplus q) \wedge r \rightarrow p \wedge r$

   (b) Show that $\sqrt{5}$ is irrational using the proof by contradiction. **5**

   (c) If A={a,b,c} and B={x,y,z} find:
   (i) A×B **2**
   (ii) A×A **2**
   (iii) A×ϕ **1**

   (d) Find the regular expression for the language:
   L={aa,aba,abba,abbba,....} **3**

   (e) Give one difference between Deterministic Finite Automata and
   Non-deterministic Finite Automata. **2**

   (f) Find the order and degree of the following recurrence relations: **3**
   (i) $a_n = a_{n-1} + a_{n-2}$
   (ii) $a_n = \sqrt{a_{n-1}} + a_{n-2}^{2}$

   (g) Determine the number of integer solutions of the equation: **4**
   $x_1 + x_2 + x_3 + x_4 = 7$, where $x_i \geq 0$ *for all* $i = 1,2,3,4$

   (h) How many three-letter words, which have a vowel in the middle position, can be formed using the letters of the English alphabet? **3**

   (i) Consider graph $G = K_4$ on four vertices a, b, c, d. Make three sub-graphs of graph G. **3**

   (j) Show that C_6 is a bipartite graph. **3**

   (k) Does the following graph have an Eulerian circuit? If yes, give the Eulerian circuit;
   if no, explain the reasons. **4**

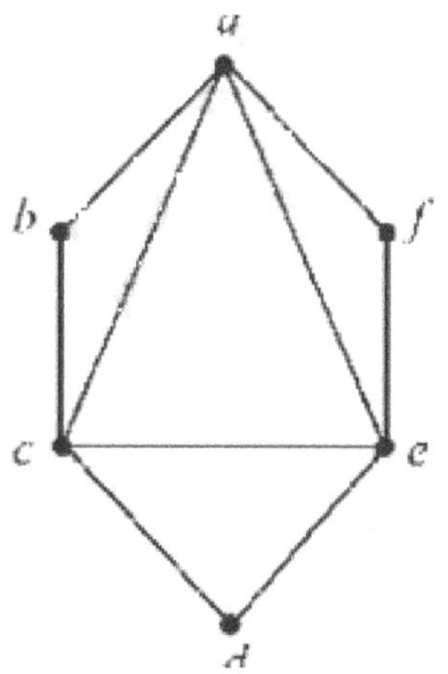

2. (a) What is a tautology? Find, if the following is a tautology:
   $[(p \rightarrow q) \wedge \sim q] \rightarrow \sim p)$ **5**

(b) Explain how the principle of mathematical induction can be used to prove: **8**
$1^2 + 2^2 + 3^2 + \cdots n^2 = \frac{n}{6}(n+1)(2n+1), \forall n \in N$

(c) Find the Boolean expression for the output of the given logic circuit. **3**

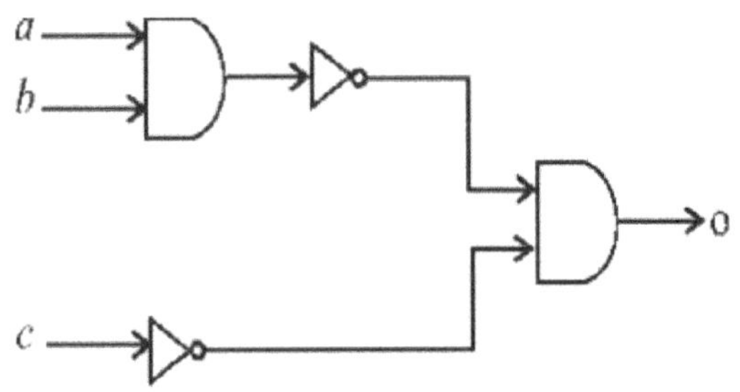

(d) Find if the following Boolean expressions are equivalent over the two-element Boolean algebra B={0,1}:
$X = (a \wedge b) \vee (a \wedge c)$ and $Y = a \wedge (b \vee c')$ **4**

3. (a) Find the power set of the set A={a,b,c,d}. **3**
(b) If A={1,2,3,4}and B={2,3,4,5,6,7} and $f: A \rightarrow B$ is defined by $f(x) = x + 1$, then find the domain and range of f. **4**
(c) If $f(x) = x^2$ and $g(x) = x + 1$, then find $fog(x)$ and $gof(x)$. **4**
(d) Explain the meaning of each symbol in the finite automata definition $M = (Q, \Sigma, \delta, q_0, F)$ **3**
(e) Consider the following finite automata:

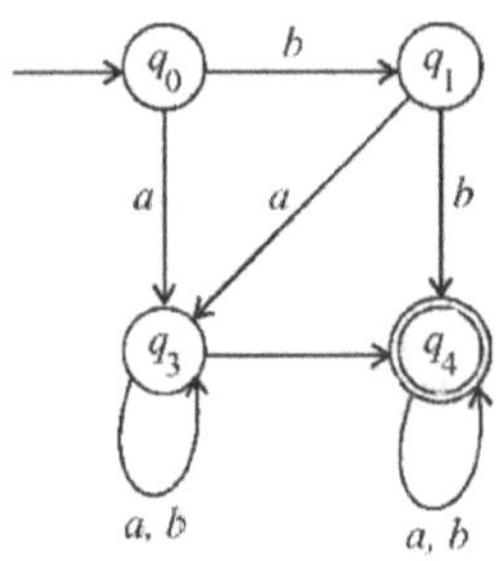

(i) What would be the values of $Q, \Sigma, \delta, q0, F$ for the automata given above? **3**
(ii) Give one string that will be accepted and one string that will not be accepted by this finite automata. **3**

4. (a) If there are 7 men and 5 women, how many circular arrangements are possible in which women do not sit adjacent to each other? **5**
(b) What is the probability that a number between 1 to 1,000 is divisible by neither 2, nor 3, nor 5? **5**
(c) What is the meaning of 'distributions' of objects? Explain with the help of an example. **5**
(d) Explain the Fibonacci numbers. Also, explain the recurrence relation for Fibonacci numbers. **5**

5. (a) Define the following terms in the context of a graph, with the help of an example:
(i) Digraph **2**
(ii) Complete graph of three vertices **2**
(iii) Degree of a vertex **2**
(iv) A regular graph **2**
(b) Explain the terms tree and forest in the context of graphs, with the help of an example. **5**
(c) What are Hamiltonian graphs? Explain with the help of an example. **5**
(d) State the travelling salesperson problem. **2**

Master Of Computer Applications (MCA)
Chapter 2: Term-End Examination, June 2022
MCS-212: Discrete Mathematics

Time: 3 Hours
Maximum Marks: 100
Note: Question No. 1 is compulsory and carries 40 marks.
Attempt any three questions from Questions No. 2 to 5.

1. (a) Write the mathematical notation for the following: **4**
   (i) The set of all odd numbers
   (ii) The set of all natural numbers whose square is more than 26.

   (b) Assuming that p and q are two propositions, find if the following two statements are logically equivalent or not by constructing the truth table: **5**

   $$\neg(p \vee q) \vee \neg q \text{ and } (p \vee \neg q) \vee q$$

   (c) Use the principle of mathematical induction to prove that: $1 + 2 + 3 + \cdots + n = \frac{n(n+1)}{2}$ for each n ∈ N. **5**

   (d) Define the term "regular expression" with the help of an example. **5**

   (e) How many different permutations are possible of the letters, taken all at a time, of the word: **ASSESSES**? **3**

   (f) A die is rolled once. What are the probabilities of the following events: **4**
   (i) Getting an odd number.
   (ii) Getting at least a value of 2.
   (iii) Getting at most a value of 2.
   (iv) Getting at least 7.

   (g) Define the problem of the Tower of Hanoi. Explain the recurrence relation to solve this problem. **6**

   (h) Draw a hypercube graph Q_3 (also called the cubical hypercube). **3**

   (i) Find if the following graphs $G_1 and\ G_2$ are isomorphic or not. **5**
   Explain how you arrived at your answer.

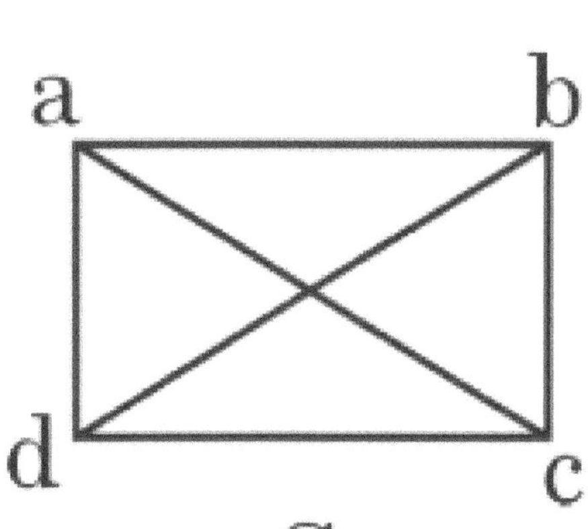

G_1

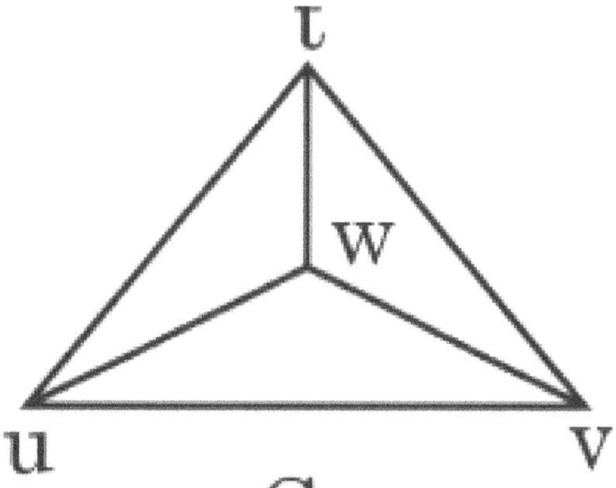

G_2

2. (a) Define the degree and order of a recurrence relation. Find the degree and order of the following recurrence relations:

(i) $a_n = {a_{n-1}}^2 + a_{n-2}\, a_{n-3} a_{n-4}$

(ii) $a_n = na_{n-2} + 2^n$ **3**

(b) What is finite automata? Why is it needed? How is finite automata represented? Explain with the help of an example. **8**

(c) What is the divide-and-conquer approach? Explain how this approach can be used to apply binary search in a sorted list. **6**

3. (a) What is a proposition? Explain with the help of an example. Explain Disjunction and Conjunction with the help of truth tables for each. **6**

(b) Prove the following theorem by direct proof method:
"The square of an even integer is an even integer." **6**

(c) Given the Boolean expression: **8**
$(a' \vee (b \wedge c')) \wedge (b \vee d')$
draw the corresponding circuit, where a,b,c and d are the inputs to the circuitry.

4. (a) Show the intersection and difference operations on two sets using Venn diagrams. **4**

(b) Define the terms Domain, Co-domain, and Range in the context of a function. Also, find the domain, co-domain, and range for a function from set A to set B, where A={1,2,3,4} and B={1,4,9,16,25} **6**

(c) A committee consisting of 2 male and 2 female workers is to be constituted from 8 male and 9 female workers. In how many distinct ways can this be done? **4**

(d) Show, using the pigeonhole principle, that in any group of 30 people, 5 people can always be found who were born on the same day of the week. **3**

(e) Find how many four-digit numbers are even. **3**

5. (a) Define the following in the context of graphs, with the help of an example: **6**

(i) Complete graph (2 marks)
(ii) Star topology (2 marks)
(iii) Degree of a vertex (2 marks)

(b) Find the complement of the following graph: **5**

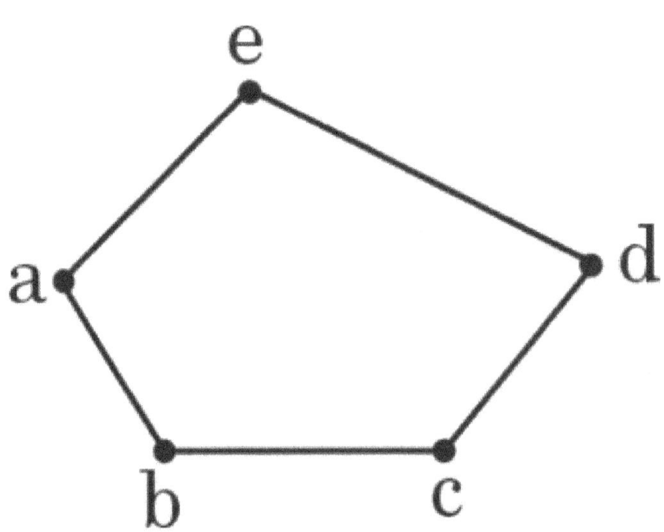

(c) What is a bipartite graph? Explain with the help of an example. **4**

(d) Differentiate between Eulerian graph and Eulerian circuit. Find the Eulerian circuit in the following graph, if it exists. **5**

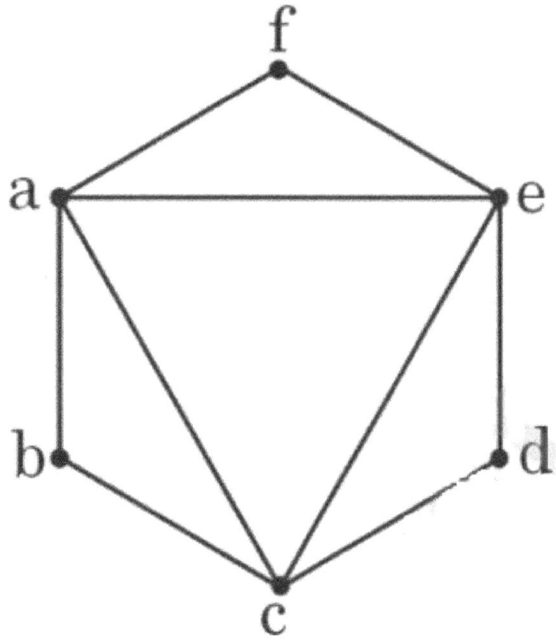

Master Of Computer Applications (MCA)
Chapter 3: Term-End Examination, December 2022
MCS-212: Discrete Mathematics

Time: 3 Hours
Maximum Marks: 100
Note: Question No. 1 is compulsory
Attempt any three questions from Questions No. 2 to 5.

1. (a) Differentiate between predicate and proposition. Also, write De Morgan's laws for both. **5**
   (b) Use De Morgan's law to derive an AND gate from a NOR gate. **5**
   (c) Explain the conditions for a relation to be an equivalence relation. **5**
   (d) Prove that $S^* = (S^*)^* = S^{**}$, where S is a set of strings. **5**
   (e) Briefly discuss a non-deterministic Turing machine. **5**
   (f) What is the addition principle? Use the addition principle to solve the following case:
   "Say there are three political parties P_1, P_2 *and* P_3 having 4, 5, and 6 members respectively."
   In how many ways can we select two persons from the same party to become President and Vice President? **5**
   (g) What is a power set? Find the power set for the following given sets:
   (i) A={0,1,3,5}
   (ii) B={ϕ,A,B,C,E} **5**
   (h) Briefly discuss the Pigeonhole principle with a suitable example. **5**

2. (a) Using induction, verify: $\sqrt{5}f_n = \left[\frac{1+\sqrt{5}}{2}\right]^n - \left[\frac{1-\sqrt{5}}{2}\right]^n \quad n \geq 1$ **5**
   (b) Define "Stirling number of the second kind." Calculate S_3^2 *and* S_4^2 **5**
   (c) Explain the Handshaking theorem with a suitable example. **5**
   (d) What is a spanning tree? Can we have a unique spanning tree?
   Draw three spanning trees for the graph given below: **5**

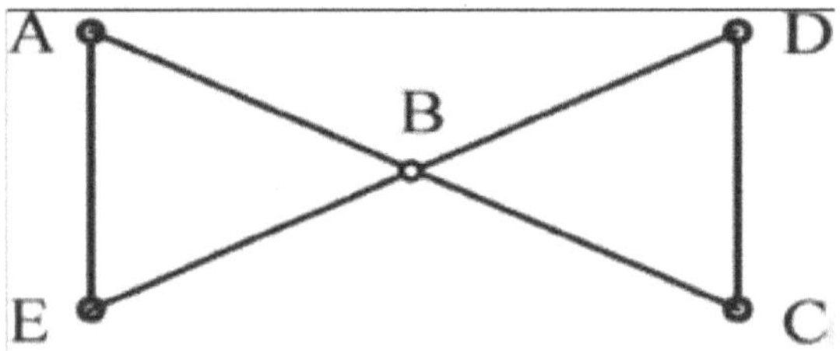

3. (a) For any two propositions x and y, verify that:
   $\neg(x \vee y) = \neg x \wedge \neg y$ **5**
   (b) Find the number of three-letter words that can be formed using the letters of the English alphabet. How many of them end in 'x'? How many of them have a vowel in the middle position? **7**
   (c) What is a regular expression? Find a regular expression to describe each of the following languages: **2+3+3**
   (i) {a,b,c}
   (ii) {λ,a,abb,abbbb,...}

4. (a) Differentiate between the following:

(i) Deterministic finite automata and Non-deterministic finite automata **5**

(ii) Moore machines and Mealy machines **5**

(b) Briefly discuss the Halting problem. **5**

(c) A box contains 3 red, 3 blue, and 4 white balls. In how many ways can 8 balls be drawn out of the box, one at a time provided order is important? **5**

5. (a) Determine the recurrence relation and iterative relation for the power set $p\ (S)$ of a set 'S'. **10**

(b) Write short notes on the following: **2*5=10**

(i) Path in a graph
(ii) Circuits in a graph
(iii) Cycles in a graph
(iv) Degree of a vertex
(v) Regularity of graph

Master Of Computer Applications (MCA)
Chapter 4: Term-End Examination, June 2023
MCS-212: Discrete Mathematics

Time: 3 Hours
Maximum Marks: 100
Note: Question No. 1 is compulsory
Attempt any three questions from Questions No. 2 to 5.

1. (a) Verify that $(a \wedge b) \wedge \sim a$ is a contradiction and $(a \rightarrow b) \leftrightarrow (\neg a \vee b)$ is a tautology. **5**
(b) Reduce the Boolean expression $(X_1 \wedge X_2) \vee (X_1 \wedge X'_2)$ to its simplest form. **5**
(c) Find the inverse of the function $f(x) = x^3 - 3$. **5**
(d) What is Kleene closure? Find Kleene closure for $\Sigma=\{0,1\}$. **5**
(e) What is the multiplication principle? Use it to find the number of ways to choose two persons as President and Vice President from a party of 35 members. **5**
(f) Briefly discuss the Inclusion-Exclusion principle with a suitable example. **5**
(g) What is an Eulerian graph? Explain with the help of a suitable diagram. **5**
(h) What is Tautology? Show that the given expression is a tautology:
$[(p \rightarrow q) \wedge \sim q] \rightarrow \sim p$ **5**

2. (a) Using induction, show that: $T_n = 2^n - 1, n \geq 1$ **5**
(b) In how many ways can 20 employees be assembled into 3 groups? **5**
(c) Explain isomorphic graphs with a suitable example. **5**
(d) What are Bipartite graphs? Show that C_6 is a Bipartite graph. **5**

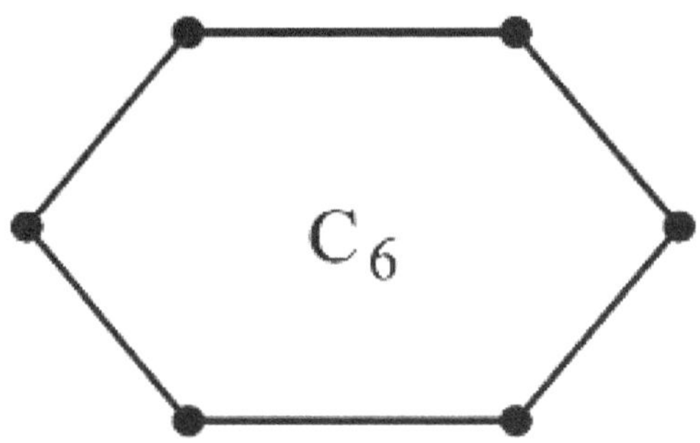

3. (a) Check whether $(\sim p \vee q) and\ p \rightarrow q$ are logically equivalent. **5**
(b) What is the chromatic number of a graph? Draw a graph with chromatic number 5. **5**
(c) Write short notes on the following:
(i) Hamiltonian Graph
(ii) Vertex Cover Problem **10**

4. (a) Show that the number of words of length 'n' on an alphabet for 'm' letters is m^n **5**
(b) Construct the logic circuit and truth table for the given expression:
$x_1 \vee (x'_2 \wedge x_3)$ **5 + 5**
(c) Given two switches, a battery, and a bulb, design the Boolean circuit for AND gate . and OR gate. **5**

5. (a) Briefly discuss the following with suitable examples for each:

(i) Finite Automata

(ii) Regular expression **5**

(b) Differentiate between Turing Acceptable Language and Turing Decidable Language. **5**

(c) If C_n is the number of comparisons required to sort a list of n integers, determine the recurrence relation and iterative relation for C_n **10**

Master Of Computer Applications (MCA)

Chapter 5: Term-End Examination, December 2023

MCS-212: Discrete Mathematics

Time: 3 Hours
Maximum Marks: 100
Note: Question No. 1 is compulsory
Attempt any three questions from Questions No. 2 to 5.

1. **(a)** Apply the precedence rules and write the truth table for the expression:
$p \rightarrow q \wedge \sim r \leftrightarrow (r \oplus q)$ **4**

(b) Show that $[(p \rightarrow q) \wedge \sim q] \rightarrow \sim p]$ is a tautology without using a truth table. **4**

(c) What is Dynamic Programming? Write four major steps involved in dynamic programming. **4**

(d) Explain Conjunctive Normal Form (CNF) with a suitable example. **4**

(e) Find the inverse of the function:

$$f(x) = \frac{x-2}{x-3}$$ **4**

(f) What is Kleene closure? Write Kleene closure for the following set of alphabets:
(i) Σ={aa,b}
(ii) Σ={a,ba} **4**

(g) What is a Turing machine? Discuss the elements of the six-tuple form of the Turing machine (Half State Version). **4**

(h) Suppose A and B are mutually exclusive events such that P(A)=0.3 and P(B)=0.4. What is the probability that:
(i) A or B occurs
(ii) Either A or B does not occur **4**

(i) State Pigeonhole principle and Inclusion-Exclusion principle. **4**

(j) Write and prove the Handshaking theorem. **4**

2. **(a)** Write down the statement "If it is raining and the rain implies that no one can go to play the match, then no one can go to play the match" as a compound proposition. Show that this proposition is a tautology by using the principles of logical equivalence. **7**

(b) Write Floyd Warshall's algorithm and apply it to find the shortest path for the graph given below (starting from vertex 1): **8**

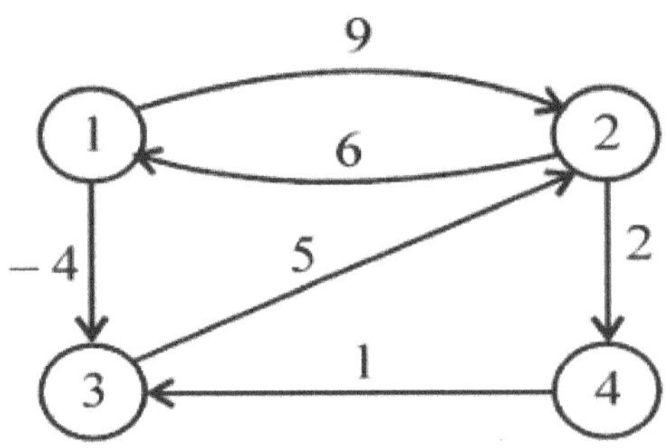

(c) Realize Conjunction, Disjunction, and Negation (i.e., AND, OR, and NOT) operations using switches. Also, write the truth table for each. **5**

3. **(a)** If A is a set with n elements, then prove that $|P(A)| = 2^n$, where P(A) is the power set of A. **5**

(b) Compare Moore and Mealy machines. **5**

(c) What is a Turing Machine? Explain the working of the constituent components of the Turing machine with the help of a block diagram. **10**

4. **(a)** Suppose we have three teams T_1, T_2 *and* T_3 Team T_1 has 4 members, T_2 has 5 members, and T_3 has 6 members in a competition. Suppose we want to select two persons from the same team, to become captain and vice-captain for each team. In how many ways can this be done? **5**

(b) Suppose 5 points are chosen at random within or on the boundary of an equilateral triangle of side 1 meter. Use the Pigeonhole principle to show that we can find two points at a distance of at most 1/2 meter. **5**

(c) Discuss the application of the Inclusion-Exclusion principle for finding the number of derangements with a suitable example. **5**

(d) Given the recurrence relation $C_n = C_{n-1} + (n-1)$ with the boundary condition $C_2 = 0$, show that: $C_n = \frac{n(n-1)}{2}$ where C_n is the number of comparisons required to sort a list of n integers. **5**

5. Explain any five of the following with suitable examples for each: **5 × 4 = 20**

(i) Bipartite graph and its applications
(ii) Circuits and cycles in a graph
(iii) Edge connectivity and Edge traceability
(iv) Hamiltonian graph and Ore's criterion
(v) Travelling salesman problem
(vi) Planar graphs

Chapter 6: Most Asked Questions Part-A

1. What is Discrete Mathematics and why is it important in computer science?
Answer: Discrete Mathematics is the branch of mathematics dealing with discrete elements that use algebra and arithmetic. It includes topics such as logic, set theory, combinatorics, graph theory, and algorithms. Unlike continuous mathematics, discrete mathematics focuses on countable, distinct structures. In computer science, it provides foundational tools for developing algorithms, data structures, cryptography, databases, and automata theory. It enables precise modeling of problems and efficient computation, forming the theoretical backbone of computing.

2. Explain the difference between a set and a multiset.
Answer: A set is a collection of distinct elements, meaning each element can occur only once. For example, {1, 2, 3} is a set. In contrast, a multiset allows for multiple occurrences of the same element. For instance, {1, 2, 2, 3} is a multiset where 2 appears twice. In computer applications, multisets are useful in contexts like inventory systems or frequency analysis, where the quantity of items matters, while sets are useful when uniqueness is important.

3. What is the principle of mathematical induction?
Answer: The principle of mathematical induction is a proof technique used to establish the truth of an infinite sequence of propositions. It consists of two steps: the base case and the inductive step. First, the base case shows the statement is true for an initial value, often $n = 0$ or $n = 1$. Second, the inductive step assumes the statement holds for $n = k$ and then proves it also holds for $n = k+1$. This method is widely used to prove statements involving natural numbers.

4. Define a function and its types in discrete mathematics.
Answer: A function in discrete mathematics is a relation between a set of inputs and a set of permissible outputs such that each input is related to exactly one output. Functions can be of various types: injective (one-to-one), surjective (onto), bijective (both one-to-one and onto), and constant functions. Functions are crucial in computer science for mapping data, defining algorithms, and modeling real-world computations.

5. What is a relation? Describe its properties.
Answer: A relation is a subset of a Cartesian product of two sets, representing how elements from one set relate to elements of another (or the same) set. A relation R on a set A has properties such as reflexivity (aRa for all a in A), symmetry (if aRb, then bRa), antisymmetry (if aRb and bRa, then a = b), and transitivity (if aRb and bRc, then aRc). Relations are foundational in database design, logic, and automata.

6. Differentiate between a graph and a tree in discrete mathematics.
Answer: A graph is a collection of nodes (vertices) connected by edges. Graphs can be directed or undirected and may contain cycles. A tree is a special type of undirected graph that is connected and acyclic, meaning there is exactly one path between any two vertices. Trees have hierarchical structures with a root node and are widely used in data structures (like binary trees) and algorithms such as search and sort.

7. What is the pigeonhole principle? Give an example.
Answer: The pigeonhole principle states that if n items are put into m containers, and if $n > m$, then at least one container must contain more than one item. For example, if you have 13 pairs of socks but only 12 drawers, at least one drawer will contain more than one pair. This principle is used in proofs and logic problems to demonstrate inevitability or redundancy.

8. Explain the concept of permutations and combinations.
Answer: Permutations and combinations are methods of counting arrangements or selections from a set. A permutation is an ordered arrangement of items, and the number of permutations of n items taken r at a time is $nPr = n! / (n-r)!$. A combination is a selection of items without considering order, and its formula is $nCr = n! / (r!(n-r)!)$. These concepts are vital in probability, algorithms, and cryptography.

9. What is Boolean algebra and how is it used in computing?
Answer: Boolean algebra is a mathematical structure that deals with binary variables and logical operations such as AND, OR, and NOT. It forms the basis of digital logic design and is used in designing circuits, programming conditional statements, and simplifying logical expressions. Boolean functions model true/false decisions in computational logic, making it essential for computer engineering and software development.

10. Define a lattice in discrete mathematics.
Answer: A lattice is a partially ordered set (poset) in which every two elements have a unique least upper bound (called join) and greatest lower bound (called meet). Lattices appear in various areas such as algebra, order theory, and logic. In computing, they are used in data classification, access control models, and formal verification. A well-known example is the power set of a set ordered by subset inclusion.

11. What is a partially ordered set (poset)? Provide an example.
Answer: A partially ordered set, or poset, is a set equipped with a partial order—a binary relation that is reflexive (every element is related to itself), antisymmetric (if $a \leq b$ and $b \leq a$, then $a = b$), and transitive (if $a \leq b$ and $b \leq c$, then $a \leq c$). However, not every pair of elements must be comparable. For example, the set of subsets of {1, 2, 3} ordered by inclusion ($\subseteq$) is a poset. Posets are useful in organizing data hierarchically and are widely used in scheduling, lattice theory, and formal concept analysis.

12. Describe the inclusion-exclusion principle in set theory.
Answer: The inclusion-exclusion principle is used to calculate the size of the union of overlapping sets by subtracting the overcounted intersections. For two sets A and B:
$|A \cup B| = |A| + |B| - |A \cap B|$
For three sets A, B, and C:
$|A \cup B \cup C| = |A| + |B| + |C| - |A \cap B| - |B \cap C| - |C \cap A| + |A \cap B \cap C|$
This principle is essential in combinatorics and probability for accurately counting elements in complex scenarios.

13. What is a Hasse diagram and how is it used?
Answer: A Hasse diagram is a graphical representation of a finite partially ordered set. In this diagram, elements are represented as vertices, and a line segment (or edge) connects two elements if one covers the other in the ordering, with edges pointing upward to represent increasing order. Hasse diagrams eliminate transitive edges for clarity. They are used in order theory, lattice theory, and visualization of hierarchical relationships in structured data.

14. Explain the concept of transitive closure of a relation.
Answer: The transitive closure of a relation R on a set A is the smallest transitive relation that contains R. In other words, if aRb and bRc, then the transitive closure also includes aRc. It's denoted as R^+. This concept is important in computer science, especially in database query processing and graph theory (e.g., determining reachability in directed graphs).

15. What is the difference between finite and infinite sets? Give examples.
Answer: A finite set contains a countable number of elements, while an infinite set has an uncountable or never-ending number of elements. For example, the set of vowels in the English alphabet {a, e, i, o, u} is finite, whereas the set of natural numbers {1, 2, 3, ...} is infinite. Understanding the distinction is important for algorithm design, as infinite sets may require different treatment in computation and logic.

16. What are graphs in discrete mathematics and their types?
Answer: A graph is a structure made of vertices (nodes) and edges (connections between nodes). Graphs can be undirected or directed (digraphs), weighted or unweighted, simple (no loops or multiple edges), or multigraphs (with loops and multiple edges). Specialized types include trees, bipartite graphs, complete graphs, and planar graphs. Graphs are fundamental in computer science for modeling networks, relationships, and pathways.

17. Explain Eulerian and Hamiltonian paths in graph theory.
Answer: An Eulerian path in a graph visits every edge exactly once, and an Eulerian circuit is an Eulerian path that starts and ends at the same vertex. A graph has an Eulerian circuit if all vertices have even degree. A Hamiltonian path visits every vertex exactly once, and a Hamiltonian cycle starts and ends at the same vertex. These concepts are used in routing problems, such as the famous "Seven Bridges of Königsberg" and the Traveling Salesman Problem.

18. What is a binary tree and what are its properties?
Answer: A binary tree is a hierarchical data structure in which each node has at most two children, referred to as the left and right child. Key properties include: the number of nodes at level l is at most 2^l, a binary tree of height h has at most 2^(h+1) − 1 nodes, and in a full binary tree, every node has 0 or 2 children. Binary trees are widely used in searching (binary search tree), sorting (heap), and expression evaluation (expression tree).

19. Define recurrence relations and give an example.
Answer: A recurrence relation is an equation that recursively defines a sequence, where each term is a function of preceding terms. For example, the Fibonacci sequence is defined by:
$F(n) = F(n-1) + F(n-2)$, with $F(0) = 0$ and $F(1) = 1$.
Recurrence relations are important in analyzing recursive algorithms and determining time complexities, such as in merge sort and binary search.

20. What is the difference between deterministic and non-deterministic finite automata?
Answer: A deterministic finite automaton (DFA) has exactly one transition for each symbol from every state, ensuring a single computation path for a given input string. A non-deterministic finite automaton (NFA) can have multiple transitions for the same symbol or even transitions without input (ε-transitions), leading to multiple possible computation paths. Although NFAs and DFAs are theoretically equivalent in expressive power, DFAs are typically more practical for implementation.

21. What is a tautology in propositional logic? Explain with an example.
Answer: A tautology is a propositional formula that is always true, regardless of the truth values of its individual components. In logic, a tautology represents a universally valid statement. For example, the statement **P ∨ ¬P** (law of the excluded middle) is a tautology because either a proposition is true, or its negation is true. Tautologies are essential in proving the validity of logical arguments and constructing truth tables.

22. Explain the pigeonhole principle with a real-life example.
Answer: The pigeonhole principle states that if *n* items are put into *m* containers and $n > m$, then at least one container must contain more than one item. A common example is with socks: if you have 13 socks and 12 drawers, at least one drawer must hold more than one sock. This principle is useful in proofs and combinatorics to demonstrate that duplicates or repetitions must exist under certain conditions.

23. What is the principle of mathematical induction? How is it applied?
Answer: Mathematical induction is a proof technique used to establish the truth of a statement for all natural numbers. It consists of two steps:
Base Case: Prove the statement for the initial value (usually n = 1).
Inductive Step: Assume the statement holds for some *k*, and then prove it holds for *k + 1*.
If both steps are successful, the statement is proven for all natural numbers. It's used to prove formulas, inequalities, and algorithm correctness.

24. Define and differentiate between injective, surjective, and bijective functions.
Answer:
Injective (One-to-One): A function f is injective if no two different elements in the domain map to the same element in the codomain.
Surjective (Onto): f is surjective if every element in the codomain has a pre-image in the domain.
Bijective: A function that is both injective and surjective, meaning it establishes a one-to-one correspondence between the domain and codomain.
These classifications are vital in understanding function properties and invertibility.

25. What are the basic properties of set operations?
Answer: The fundamental properties of set operations include:
Commutativity: A ∪ B = B ∪ A, A ∩ B = B ∩ A
Associativity: (A ∪ B) ∪ C = A ∪ (B ∪ C)
Distributivity: A ∩ (B ∪ C) = (A ∩ B) ∪ (A ∩ C)
Identity Laws: A ∪ ∅ = A, A ∩ U = A

Complement Laws: A ∪ A' = U, A ∩ A' = ∅
These help simplify and prove expressions in set theory and logic.

26. What is the adjacency matrix of a graph and how is it used?
Answer: An adjacency matrix is a square matrix used to represent a finite graph. For a graph with n vertices, it is an $n \times n$ matrix where the element at row i, column j is 1 if there is an edge from vertex i to vertex j, and 0 otherwise. For weighted graphs, weights replace the 1s. This matrix helps in determining paths, connectivity, and is used in algorithms like Floyd-Warshall for shortest paths.

27. Explain Boolean algebra and its applications.
Answer: Boolean algebra is a branch of algebra that deals with variables that take values true or false (1 or 0) and logical operations such as AND (·), OR (+), and NOT ('). It follows specific laws like identity, distributive, and DeMorgan's laws. Boolean algebra is the foundation of digital electronics and is used in designing circuits, simplifying logic gates, and creating truth tables.

28. What is a spanning tree in graph theory?
Answer: A spanning tree of a connected undirected graph is a subgraph that includes all the vertices and is a tree (i.e., it is acyclic and connected). A graph can have multiple spanning trees. Spanning trees are critical in network design, where you want to ensure all nodes are connected with minimal cost and no cycles, such as in internet routing and utility networks.

29. Define Lattice in the context of partially ordered sets.
Answer: A lattice is a poset in which every pair of elements has a unique least upper bound (join) and greatest lower bound (meet). Formally, for any a and b in the lattice, both a ∨ b (join) and a ∧ b (meet) exist. Lattices are widely used in algebra, logic, and computer science, especially in abstract data type theory and information flow analysis.

30. What is the difference between a path and a cycle in graph theory?
Answer: In graph theory, a **path** is a sequence of vertices such that each adjacent pair is connected by an edge, and no vertex is repeated. A **cycle** is a path where the first and last vertices are the same, and no other vertices are repeated. Paths and cycles are central in analyzing connectivity and designing algorithms such as DFS, BFS, and detecting deadlocks in systems.

31. What is the Hasse diagram, and how is it used in discrete mathematics?
Answer: A Hasse diagram is a graphical representation of a finite partially ordered set (poset). In this diagram, each element is represented by a vertex, and edges are drawn to indicate the order relation between elements, omitting transitive and reflexive relations for clarity. The diagram is drawn so that if element **a ≤ b**, then **a** appears lower than **b**. Hasse diagrams are useful in visualizing ordering relationships, lattice structures, and hierarchical data in set theory and algebra.

32. Explain the principle of inclusion and exclusion in combinatorics.
Answer: The principle of inclusion and exclusion is used to calculate the cardinality of the union of multiple sets by adding the sizes of individual sets and subtracting the sizes of all pairwise intersections, adding back triple-wise intersections, and so on. For two sets A and B, it is:
$|A \cup B| = |A| + |B| - |A \cap B|$
It helps solve problems where elements might be counted multiple times due to overlaps and is used extensively in probability and counting problems.

33. Define Euler circuit and Hamiltonian circuit in a graph.
Answer:
An **Euler circuit** is a cycle that traverses each edge of a graph exactly once and returns to the starting vertex. It exists only if every vertex has even degree and the graph is connected.
A **Hamiltonian circuit** is a cycle that visits each vertex exactly once and returns to the starting point, regardless of how many times edges are used.
These circuits are essential in routing problems, such as the classic "traveling salesman problem."

34. What is a generating function in combinatorics? Provide an example.
Answer: A generating function is a formal power series in which the coefficients correspond to terms in a sequence. It is used as a tool to study and solve recurrence relations and counting problems. For example, for the sequence 1, 1, 1, ..., the generating function is:
$$G(x) = 1 + x + x^2 + x^3 + ... = 1 / (1 - x)$$
They are powerful in deriving closed-form expressions and solving partition problems in combinatorics.

35. What are equivalence relations? Give an example.
Answer: An equivalence relation on a set is a relation that is reflexive, symmetric, and transitive. It partitions the set into disjoint equivalence classes where elements are considered equivalent under some condition.
Example: On set of integers Z, define relation R such that a R b if $a \equiv b \pmod 3$. This relation is:
Reflexive: $a \equiv a \bmod 3$
Symmetric: if $a \equiv b$, then $b \equiv a$
Transitive: if $a \equiv b$ and $b \equiv c$, then $a \equiv c$
Equivalence relations are foundational in classification, modular arithmetic, and quotient sets.

36. Define and explain recurrence relations with an example.
Answer: A recurrence relation is an equation that defines each term of a sequence as a function of its preceding terms. For instance, the Fibonacci sequence is defined by the recurrence relation:
$$F(n) = F(n-1) + F(n-2), \text{ with } F(0) = 0, F(1) = 1$$
Recurrence relations appear in algorithm analysis (e.g., divide-and-conquer), counting problems, and dynamic programming.

37. Explain the concept of graph coloring and its applications.
Answer: Graph coloring involves assigning colors to the vertices of a graph such that no two adjacent vertices share the same color. The minimum number of colors needed is called the **chromatic number**.
Applications include:
Scheduling problems (e.g., exam timetables)
Map coloring
Register allocation in compilers
It helps in solving problems where conflict-free assignments are needed.

38. What is a directed acyclic graph (DAG) and where is it used?
Answer: A Directed Acyclic Graph (DAG) is a finite directed graph with no cycles. That means it's impossible to start at a node and return to it by following directed edges. DAGs are widely used in:
Representing tasks in scheduling
Dependency resolution (like package installations)
Topological sorting
In computer science, DAGs are crucial for representing data flow and managing precedence constraints.

39. Describe DeMorgan's Laws in Boolean algebra.
Answer: DeMorgan's Laws relate the logical operators AND and OR with NOT. They state:
$$\neg(A \land B) = \neg A \lor \neg B$$
$$\neg(A \lor B) = \neg A \land \neg B$$
These laws are useful in simplifying logic circuits and expressions in Boolean algebra and are foundational in digital electronics and programming conditions.

40. What are permutations and combinations? Differentiate with examples.
Answer:
Permutations refer to arrangements of objects where order matters. The number of permutations of *r* objects from *n* is $nPr = n! / (n-r)!$
Combinations refer to selections where order does not matter. The number of combinations is $nCr = n! / [r!(n-r)!]$
Example: From 3 letters A, B, C:
Permutations of 2: AB, BA, AC, CA, BC, CB
Combinations of 2: AB, AC, BC
They are used in probability, statistics, and various optimization problems.

41. Explain the concept of mathematical induction and its applications.
Answer: Mathematical induction is a proof technique used to establish the truth of an infinite sequence of statements, typically indexed by natural numbers. It involves two steps:
Base Case: Prove the statement is true for the initial value (usually n = 1).
Inductive Step: Assume the statement is true for n = k, and then prove it for n = k + 1.
If both steps are successful, the statement is true for all natural numbers. It's widely used to prove formulas, divisibility, inequalities, and properties of sequences.

42. What is a lattice in discrete mathematics? Provide an example.
Answer: A lattice is a partially ordered set (poset) in which every pair of elements has a unique least upper bound (called join) and a greatest lower bound (called meet).
Example: The set of natural numbers under divisibility forms a lattice, where the **join** is the least common multiple (LCM) and the **meet** is the greatest common divisor (GCD).
Lattices are significant in algebra, logic, and computer science (e.g., in data classification and access control models).

43. Define bipartite graph. How can you check if a graph is bipartite?
Answer: A bipartite graph is a graph whose vertex set can be divided into two disjoint sets U and V such that every edge connects a vertex in U to one in V. No edge connects vertices within the same set.
To check if a graph is bipartite, you can use BFS or DFS to attempt to color the graph using two colors. If successful (i.e., no two adjacent vertices share the same color), the graph is bipartite. These graphs are used in matching problems, scheduling, and recommendation systems.

44. What is the pigeonhole principle? State an example.
Answer: The pigeonhole principle states that if **n** items are put into **m** containers and **n** > **m**, then at least one container must contain more than one item.
Example: If there are 13 people in a room, at least two of them must have their birthdays in the same month.
This principle is used in proofs involving existence and in probability, combinatorics, and hashing algorithms.

45. Describe the difference between simple graphs, multigraphs, and pseudographs.
Answer:
Simple Graph: A graph with no loops or multiple edges between the same pair of vertices.
Multigraph: A graph that may have multiple edges (parallel edges) between the same vertices but no loops.
Pseudograph: A graph that can have both loops and multiple edges.
These classifications help define constraints in modeling networks like transportation, communication, and social networks.

46. What is a power set? How many elements does it contain?
Answer: The power set of a set S is the set of all possible subsets of S, including the empty set and S itself. If S has **n** elements, the power set has $\mathbf{2^n}$ elements.
Example: If S = {a, b}, then Power Set = {∅, {a}, {b}, {a, b}}.
Power sets are fundamental in set theory, logic, and probability, representing all possible outcomes or choices.

47. What is meant by the term isomorphism in graphs?
Answer: Two graphs G and H are said to be isomorphic if there exists a one-to-one correspondence between their vertices such that adjacency is preserved. That is, if vertex **u** is connected to **v** in G, their corresponding vertices in H are also connected.
Isomorphic graphs have the same number of vertices and edges, and the same degree sequence. Graph isomorphism helps identify structurally equivalent graphs, even if they appear different visually.

48. Explain the difference between tautology, contradiction, and contingency in logic.
Answer:
Tautology: A logical statement that is always true, regardless of the truth values of its components (e.g., **P ∨ ¬P**).
Contradiction: A statement that is always false (e.g., **P ∧ ¬P**).

Contingency: A statement that is sometimes true and sometimes false, depending on the truth values of its components.
These distinctions are key in propositional logic, circuit design, and logical reasoning.

49. Define the term transitive closure of a relation with an example.
Answer: The transitive closure of a relation R on a set A is the smallest transitive relation R^+ that contains R. It includes all indirect paths implied by R.
Example: If R = {(a, b), (b, c)}, then R^+ includes (a, c) because a is related to c through b.
It's crucial in database query systems, graph algorithms (e.g., reachability), and knowledge representation.

50. What is a spanning tree? Mention one algorithm to find it.
Answer: A spanning tree of a connected undirected graph is a subgraph that includes all the vertices of the original graph and is a tree (i.e., it has no cycles and minimum number of edges). It connects all vertices with the minimum possible edges (n−1 for n vertices).
Kruskal's Algorithm and **Prim's Algorithm** are common methods to find minimum spanning trees, used in network design, circuit layout, and clustering.

51. What is meant by equivalence relation? List its properties.
Answer: An equivalence relation on a set is a relation that satisfies the following three properties:
Reflexive: For all a in A, (a, a) ∈ R.
Symmetric: If (a, b) ∈ R, then (b, a) ∈ R.
Transitive: If (a, b) ∈ R and (b, c) ∈ R, then (a, c) ∈ R.
An equivalence relation partitions the set into disjoint equivalence classes. For example, "has the same remainder when divided by 3" is an equivalence relation on integers.

52. What is a Boolean algebra? Give an example.
Answer: Boolean algebra is a mathematical structure that deals with binary variables and logical operations. It includes operations like AND (·), OR (+), and NOT ('), and satisfies specific identities like distributive, commutative, and De Morgan's laws.
Example: The set {0,1} with operations AND, OR, and NOT forms a Boolean algebra. Boolean algebra is fundamental in logic circuits, switching theory, and computer design.

53. Explain the concept of Hasse diagrams.
Answer: A Hasse diagram is a graphical representation of a finite partially ordered set (poset), where elements are represented as vertices and the order relation is shown by edges going upwards without drawing transitive edges.
Hasse diagrams help visualize the structure of posets and determine upper bounds, lower bounds, maximal/minimal elements, and lattices.

54. Define Euler circuit and Euler path. Provide the conditions for their existence.
Answer:
Euler Path: A trail in a graph that visits every edge exactly once.
Euler Circuit: An Euler path that starts and ends at the same vertex.
Conditions:
A connected graph has an Euler circuit if all vertices have even degrees.
A connected graph has an Euler path (but not a circuit) if exactly two vertices have odd degrees.

55. What is a Hamiltonian cycle? How does it differ from an Eulerian cycle?
Answer: A Hamiltonian cycle is a cycle in a graph that visits each vertex exactly once and returns to the starting vertex.
Difference:
Hamiltonian Cycle: Visits all **vertices** exactly once.
Eulerian Cycle: Traverses all **edges** exactly once.
Determining Hamiltonian cycles is generally harder and is an NP-complete problem.

56. What are the basic rules of inference in propositional logic?
Answer: Rules of inference are logical rules that define valid argument forms. Common ones include:

Modus Ponens: If P → Q and P are true, then Q is true.
Modus Tollens: If P → Q and ¬Q are true, then ¬P is true.
Disjunctive Syllogism: P ∨ Q and ¬P implies Q.
These rules are foundational in proofs, algorithm correctness, and AI reasoning.

57. Explain the term cardinality of a set. How do you compare sizes of infinite sets?
Answer: Cardinality refers to the number of elements in a set.
Finite sets: Cardinality is the count of elements.
Infinite sets: Compared using bijections.
Example: The set of natural numbers (ℕ) and the set of even natural numbers have the same cardinality (countably infinite), despite one being a proper subset of the other.

58. What is a function? Differentiate between injective, surjective, and bijective functions.
Answer: A function from set A to B assigns each element in A to exactly one element in B.
Injective (One-to-One): Different inputs map to different outputs.
Surjective (Onto): Every element of B is mapped by some element in A.
Bijective: Both injective and surjective – perfect one-to-one correspondence.
These classifications are crucial in set theory, logic, and database design.

59. What is the role of recurrence relations in discrete mathematics?
Answer: Recurrence relations define sequences based on previous terms. They are used to model and analyze recursive algorithms and combinatorial problems.
Example: Fibonacci sequence – F(n) = F(n−1) + F(n−2), with base cases F(0) = 0, F(1) = 1.
Solving recurrence relations helps evaluate algorithm complexity and predict system behavior.

60. Define the chromatic number of a graph. How is it useful?
Answer: The chromatic number of a graph is the minimum number of colors needed to color its vertices so that no two adjacent vertices share the same color.
It is used in scheduling problems, register allocation in compilers, and map coloring. For example, coloring tasks so that no overlapping task is assigned the same resource.

61. What are the basic properties of equivalence relations?
Answer: The basic properties of equivalence relations are reflexivity, symmetry, and transitivity. Reflexivity ensures that every element is related to itself, i.e., for all a in a set A, (a, a) ∈ R. Symmetry means that if a is related to b, then b must also be related to a, i.e., if (a, b) ∈ R then (b, a) ∈ R. Transitivity requires that if a is related to b and b is related to c, then a must be related to c, i.e., if (a, b) ∈ R and (b, c) ∈ R then (a, c) ∈ R. These three properties ensure a well-defined equivalence relation, often used in partitioning sets into disjoint subsets called equivalence classes.

62. Explain the concept of partial order relations.
Answer: A partial order relation is a binary relation that is reflexive, antisymmetric, and transitive. Reflexivity means every element is related to itself; antisymmetry means that if a is related to b and b is related to a, then a must be equal to b; and transitivity ensures that if a is related to b and b to c, then a is related to c. A set with a partial order is known as a partially ordered set or poset. Unlike total order, not every pair of elements need be comparable in partial orders, which is useful in representing hierarchies and dependency relationships.

63. What is a Hasse diagram?
Answer: A Hasse diagram is a graphical representation of a finite partially ordered set (poset). It omits self-loops and redundant transitive edges, making the diagram more readable. In the Hasse diagram, elements are represented as vertices, and a directed edge is drawn upward from a lower element to a higher one if there is a direct relationship between them. It helps visualize the order structure by indicating which elements are immediately less than or greater than others, thus simplifying the analysis of posets, lattices, and hierarchy structures.

64. Define a lattice and its types.
Answer: A lattice is a partially ordered set in which every pair of elements has a unique least upper bound (join) and a unique greatest lower bound (meet). There are two main types of lattices: bounded and distributive. A bounded

lattice has a greatest element (top) and least element (bottom). A distributive lattice satisfies the distributive laws for meet and join, i.e., $a \wedge (b \vee c) = (a \wedge b) \vee (a \wedge c)$. Lattices are important in algebra and computer science, particularly in data structure hierarchies and formal logic.

65. What are Boolean algebras?
Answer: Boolean algebras are algebraic structures that capture the logic of binary variables and logical operations. A Boolean algebra consists of a set with two binary operations (join and meet), a unary operation (complement), and two distinct elements (0 and 1), satisfying properties such as commutativity, associativity, distributivity, identity, and complementation. They are widely used in logic circuits, digital electronics, set theory, and propositional logic. Boolean algebras model true/false values and are foundational in designing logic gates and algorithms.

66. Explain the concept of functions in discrete mathematics.
Answer: In discrete mathematics, a function is a relation that maps each element of one set (domain) to a unique element of another set (codomain). Functions are represented as $f: A \rightarrow B$, where each element in set A is associated with exactly one element in set B. Functions can be injective (one-to-one), surjective (onto), or bijective (both). Functions are fundamental in defining mathematical models, transformations, and algorithms. They play a crucial role in areas like combinatorics, logic, and computer programming.

67. What is the difference between injective, surjective, and bijective functions?
Answer: Injective functions (one-to-one) map distinct elements of the domain to distinct elements of the codomain. Surjective functions (onto) cover the entire codomain, meaning every element in the codomain has a pre-image in the domain. Bijective functions are both injective and surjective, implying a perfect one-to-one correspondence between domain and codomain elements. Understanding these types is important in function analysis, inverse function computation, and determining cardinality between sets in discrete mathematics.

68. Define recurrence relations with an example.
Answer: A recurrence relation is an equation that recursively defines a sequence, i.e., each term is defined as a function of its preceding terms. For example, the Fibonacci sequence is defined by the recurrence relation: $F(n) = F(n-1) + F(n-2)$, with initial values $F(0) = 0$ and $F(1) = 1$. Recurrence relations are used to describe the behavior of recursive algorithms, model problems in counting, and solve divide-and-conquer problems. Solving recurrence relations helps in deriving explicit formulas for sequence terms.

69. What is the method of iteration in solving recurrence relations?
Answer: The method of iteration involves repeatedly expanding a recurrence relation until a pattern emerges that allows a general expression to be formed. For example, for $T(n) = T(n-1) + 2$, with $T(1) = 1$, we expand iteratively: $T(2) = T(1) + 2 = 3$, $T(3) = T(2) + 2 = 5$, and so on, leading to the general form $T(n) = 2n - 1$. This technique is especially useful for linear recurrence relations with constant coefficients and helps in finding closed-form solutions for algorithm complexity.

70. Describe the Master Theorem in relation to recurrence relations.
Answer: The Master Theorem provides a direct way to determine the time complexity of divide-and-conquer algorithms characterized by recurrence relations of the form $T(n) = aT(n/b) + f(n)$, where $a \geq 1$ and $b > 1$. It offers three cases based on the comparison between f(n) and n^log_b(a). The theorem allows for quick identification of the growth rate (Big-O) of the recurrence without the need for iteration or recursion tree methods. It is commonly used in analyzing algorithms like Merge Sort, Quick Sort, and Binary Search.

71. What is a generating function in combinatorics?
Answer: A generating function is a formal power series where the coefficients represent a sequence of numbers. It is an analytical tool used in combinatorics to study and manipulate sequences. For a sequence $a_0, a_1, a_2, \ldots$, the generating function is $G(x) = a_0 + a_1x + a_2x^2 + \ldots$. Generating functions simplify complex counting problems, recurrence relations, and partition problems by converting them into algebraic problems that can be manipulated easily and systematically.

72. Explain the pigeonhole principle with an example.
Answer: The pigeonhole principle states that if n items are put into m containers and n > m, then at least one container must contain more than one item. For example, if 10 socks are placed in 9 drawers, at least one drawer will have more than one sock. This principle is used in proofs and problem-solving where guarantees about repetition or overlap are needed, such as in number theory, graph theory, and computer science.

73. Define a graph in discrete mathematics.
Answer: A graph is a collection of vertices (nodes) and edges (connections between vertices). It is denoted as G = (V, E), where V is the set of vertices and E is the set of edges. Graphs can be undirected or directed (digraphs), weighted or unweighted, and may contain loops or multiple edges. Graphs are widely used to model networks, relationships, and paths in computer science, logistics, social media, and more.

74. What is the difference between a simple graph and a multigraph?
Answer: A simple graph is an undirected graph that has no loops (edges connecting a vertex to itself) and no more than one edge between any two vertices. A multigraph, on the other hand, may have multiple edges (parallel edges) between the same pair of vertices and may include loops. The distinction is important for defining different graph algorithms and for modeling scenarios where multiple connections or self-links exist.

75. What is a path and a cycle in a graph?
Answer: A path in a graph is a sequence of vertices such that each pair of consecutive vertices is connected by an edge. A cycle is a path that starts and ends at the same vertex, with no other repetitions of vertices or edges. Paths and cycles are essential in graph traversal, detecting connectivity, finding shortest routes, and analyzing circuit problems.

76. Explain connected and disconnected graphs.
Answer: A connected graph is one in which there is a path between every pair of vertices. In contrast, a disconnected graph has at least one pair of vertices with no path connecting them. In directed graphs, this concept is known as strongly or weakly connected. Connectivity is crucial in network design, communication models, and determining the robustness of systems.

77. What is a tree in graph theory?
Answer: A tree is a connected, undirected graph with no cycles. It is a special kind of graph where any two vertices are connected by exactly one path. Trees are widely used in computer science for representing hierarchical structures such as file systems, decision trees, and search trees. A tree with n vertices always has n−1 edges, making it minimally connected.

78. Define a binary tree and its types.
Answer: A binary tree is a tree data structure in which each node has at most two children, called the left and right child. Types of binary trees include full binary trees (each node has 0 or 2 children), complete binary trees (all levels are filled except possibly the last), and binary search trees (left child < parent < right child). Binary trees are used in searching, sorting, expression parsing, and hierarchical data representation.

79. What is a spanning tree?
Answer: A spanning tree of a connected graph is a subgraph that includes all the vertices of the graph and is a tree (i.e., connected and acyclic). It has exactly n−1 edges if there are n vertices. Spanning trees are used in network design to reduce the number of connections while still maintaining connectivity. Minimum spanning trees, like those found by Kruskal's or Prim's algorithms, help in optimizing costs in weighted graphs.

80. Explain the concept of graph isomorphism.
Answer: Two graphs are isomorphic if there exists a one-to-one correspondence between their vertex sets and edge sets that preserves adjacency. In other words, the graphs have the same structure but may appear differently when drawn. Graph isomorphism is important in pattern recognition, chemical structure comparison, and database indexing. Determining isomorphism helps in identifying equivalent structures and redundancy.

81. What is a directed acyclic graph (DAG)?
Answer: A Directed Acyclic Graph (DAG) is a directed graph with no cycles. DAGs are used to represent processes with dependencies, such as task scheduling, data processing pipelines, and compiler optimization. They allow a topological ordering of vertices, which helps in solving problems like shortest paths and dependency resolution. DAGs are fundamental in many algorithms in computer science.

82. Describe topological sorting.
Answer: Topological sorting is the linear ordering of vertices in a directed acyclic graph (DAG) such that for every directed edge (u, v), vertex u comes before v in the ordering. It is used in scheduling tasks, course prerequisites, and build systems where some tasks must precede others. Algorithms like Kahn's and DFS-based approaches are used for topological sorting. It is only applicable to DAGs.

83. What are Eulerian paths and circuits?
Answer: An Eulerian path in a graph is a path that visits every edge exactly once, while an Eulerian circuit starts and ends at the same vertex. A graph has an Eulerian circuit if all vertices have even degree, and it has an Eulerian path if exactly zero or two vertices have odd degree. These concepts are used in route planning and graph traversal problems.

84. What are Hamiltonian paths and cycles?
Answer: A Hamiltonian path visits each vertex exactly once, while a Hamiltonian cycle is a Hamiltonian path that starts and ends at the same vertex. Unlike Eulerian paths, they concern visiting vertices rather than edges. Determining Hamiltonian paths and cycles is a computationally hard problem and has applications in optimization, like the Traveling Salesman Problem.

85. What is the principle of inclusion and exclusion?
Answer: The principle of inclusion and exclusion is a counting technique used to find the cardinality of the union of overlapping sets. It adds the sizes of individual sets, subtracts the sizes of all pairwise intersections, adds the size of triple-wise intersections, and so on. For two sets A and B: $|A \cup B| = |A| + |B| - |A \cap B|$. This principle helps solve complex counting problems involving overlaps.

86. Explain the concept of permutations and combinations.
Answer: Permutations refer to the arrangement of objects in a specific order, while combinations refer to the selection of objects regardless of order. The number of permutations of n objects taken r at a time is $nPr = n! / (n-r)!$, and the number of combinations is $nCr = n! / [r!(n-r)!]$. These concepts are essential in probability, statistics, and discrete problem-solving.

87. What is a recurrence tree?
Answer: A recurrence tree is a visual tool used to represent the breakdown of a recursive function or algorithm. Each node shows a recursive call, and its children represent the further subdivisions of that call. It helps to visualize the number of recursive calls, the depth of recursion, and the total work done. This method aids in analyzing recursive algorithms, especially those following divide-and-conquer strategies.

88. Define the concept of probability in discrete mathematics.
Answer: In discrete mathematics, probability is the measure of the likelihood that an event will occur, typically defined as the ratio of favorable outcomes to the total number of equally likely outcomes. For example, the probability of getting heads in a fair coin toss is 1/2. Discrete probability deals with countable sample spaces and is used in computer science, game theory, and algorithms.

89. What is conditional probability?
Answer: Conditional probability is the probability of an event A occurring given that another event B has occurred, denoted as $P(A|B) = P(A \cap B) / P(B)$, provided $P(B) \neq 0$. It is used in scenarios where one event influences the likelihood of another. Conditional probability is central to Bayes' theorem, decision-making, and risk assessment in statistics and machine learning.

90. Explain Bayes' theorem with a simple example.
Answer: Bayes' theorem describes the probability of an event based on prior knowledge of related conditions. It is stated as: $P(A|B) = [P(B|A) \times P(A)] / P(B)$. For example, if 1% of emails are spam and 90% of spam emails contain the word "free", Bayes' theorem helps determine the probability that an email is spam given it contains "free". It's widely used in spam filtering, medical diagnosis, and AI.

91. Explain the pigeonhole principle with an example.
Answer: The pigeonhole principle states that if more items are put into fewer containers, then at least one container must hold more than one item. Formally, if n items are placed into m containers, and $n > m$, then at least one container contains more than one item. For example, if there are 13 socks in 12 drawers, at least one drawer contains at least 2 socks. This principle is useful in proving the existence of duplicates or repetitions in sets and has wide applications in computer science, probability, and combinatorics.

92. What are permutations and combinations? How do they differ?
Answer: Permutations and combinations are techniques used to count arrangements or selections of items. Permutations refer to the number of ways to arrange a set of items where order matters, calculated as $nPr = n! / (n - r)!$. Combinations refer to the number of ways to choose items where order does not matter, calculated as $nCr = n! / [r!(n - r)!]$. For example, selecting 2 books from 3 and arranging them is permutation, while just selecting them is combination. Understanding both is crucial for solving counting problems in discrete mathematics.

93. What is mathematical induction and how is it used?
Answer: Mathematical induction is a proof technique used to establish the truth of statements about natural numbers. It consists of two steps: the base case, where the statement is verified for the initial value (usually $n = 1$), and the inductive step, where the statement is assumed true for $n = k$ and proven true for $n = k + 1$. This method helps in proving formulas, theorems, and properties involving sequences, summations, and recursively defined structures. It ensures correctness for an infinite number of cases using a finite procedure.

94. Explain the inclusion-exclusion principle.
Answer: The inclusion-exclusion principle is a method used in counting the number of elements in the union of multiple sets. It avoids over-counting by subtracting the sizes of intersections. For two sets A and B, $|A \cup B| = |A| + |B| - |A \cap B|$. For three sets A, B, and C, the formula extends by adding sizes of individual sets, subtracting pairwise intersections, and adding back the intersection of all three. This principle is used in probability, counting, and analysis of overlapping events or sets.

95. What are generating functions in discrete mathematics?
Answer: A generating function is a formal power series where the coefficients correspond to elements of a sequence. It is written as $G(x) = a_0 + a_1x + a_2x^2 + \ldots$, where a_n represents the nth term. Generating functions are used to encode sequences and solve recurrence relations. They simplify computations involving sums and sequences, and they are useful in combinatorics for deriving closed-form expressions and proving identities. They also assist in solving problems in number theory and algorithm analysis.

96. Define a graph and explain its types.
Answer: A graph is a collection of nodes (vertices) and edges that connect pairs of nodes. Graphs are classified as directed or undirected. In a directed graph (digraph), edges have a direction, while in an undirected graph, edges do not. Other classifications include simple graphs (no loops or multiple edges), multigraphs (multiple edges allowed), weighted graphs (edges have weights), and connected graphs (path exists between all pairs of vertices). Graphs model networks such as social media, computer networks, and transportation systems.

97. What is the difference between a tree and a graph?
Answer: A tree is a special type of graph that is connected and acyclic, meaning it has no cycles. A graph can be cyclic or acyclic and may not necessarily be connected. Every tree with n vertices has exactly $n - 1$ edges. Trees are hierarchical and are widely used in computer science for data structures like binary trees, heaps, and decision trees. Graphs are more general and used for modeling broader relationships, including cyclic and non-hierarchical connections like in social or road networks.

98. Explain the concept of isomorphism in graphs.
Answer: Two graphs are isomorphic if there exists a one-to-one correspondence between their vertices and edges that preserves adjacency. In other words, graph G1 is isomorphic to G2 if G1 can be transformed into G2 simply by renaming the vertices. Graph isomorphism helps determine structural similarity and is used in chemistry for comparing molecular structures, in computer vision, and in verifying equivalence of data models. Determining isomorphism is computationally challenging and still lacks a polynomial-time solution for all cases.

99. What is a spanning tree? Give its applications.
Answer: A spanning tree is a subgraph of a connected graph that includes all the vertices and is a tree (connected and acyclic). Every connected graph has at least one spanning tree. The number of spanning trees varies depending on the graph structure. Spanning trees are used in network design (e.g., minimizing cable length), optimization (like in minimum spanning tree problems), and broadcasting in computer networks. Algorithms like Kruskal's and Prim's are used to find minimum spanning trees efficiently.

100. Describe the difference between DFS and BFS traversal in graphs.
Answer: Depth-First Search (DFS) and Breadth-First Search (BFS) are graph traversal algorithms. DFS explores as far as possible along each branch before backtracking, using a stack (often recursive). BFS explores all neighbors at the current level before going deeper, using a queue. DFS is suited for tasks like topological sorting, maze solving, and cycle detection, while BFS is used in shortest path finding (in unweighted graphs), level-order traversal, and connectivity checking. Choice between them depends on the problem and graph structure.

101. What is a binary tree? Explain its properties.
Answer: A binary tree is a tree data structure in which each node has at most two children, called the left and right child. Important properties include: the number of nodes at level *l* is at most 2^l; the maximum number of nodes in a binary tree of height *h* is 2^(h+1) − 1; and in a full binary tree, every node has 0 or 2 children. Binary trees are used in searching (binary search trees), expression parsing (expression trees), and heaps.

102. What are Boolean functions? How are they represented?
Answer: Boolean functions are algebraic expressions composed of binary variables and logical operations like AND, OR, and NOT. A Boolean function takes binary inputs and produces a binary output. They can be represented using truth tables, logic circuits, or algebraic expressions. These functions are central to digital electronics, circuit design, and logic simplification. They are used in computer science for decision-making logic, programming, and automata theory.

103. Explain the difference between a tautology and a contradiction.
Answer: A tautology is a logical statement that is always true regardless of the truth values of its components. A contradiction is always false regardless of input values. For example, "P ∨ ¬P" is a tautology, while "P ∧ ¬P" is a contradiction. Tautologies are important in proving the validity of arguments, while contradictions help identify inconsistencies. Both are essential tools in propositional logic and automated reasoning.

104. What is a finite state machine (FSM)?
Answer: A finite state machine is a mathematical model of computation consisting of a finite number of states, transitions between states, and an initial state. FSMs can be deterministic (DFA) or nondeterministic (NFA). They are used to model sequential logic, control systems, lexical analyzers, and protocol design. FSMs accept regular languages and are represented using state diagrams or transition tables. They are foundational in automata theory and formal language processing.

105. What are recurrence relations? Give an example.
Answer: Recurrence relations define a sequence where each term is based on previous terms. For example, the Fibonacci sequence is defined by F(n) = F(n−1) + F(n−2) with F(0)=0, F(1)=1. Recurrence relations are used to analyze recursive algorithms and count combinatorial objects. They are solved using iteration, substitution, or

generating functions. Understanding them is crucial for analyzing time complexities and constructing mathematical models.

106. Define modular arithmetic and give its application.
Answer: Modular arithmetic deals with integers wrapped around after reaching a certain value called the modulus. It is denoted as $a \equiv b \pmod{n}$ meaning a and b leave the same remainder when divided by n. For example, $17 \equiv 2 \pmod{5}$. It is widely used in computer science for hashing, cryptography (e.g., RSA algorithm), clock arithmetic, and cyclic structures. Its properties simplify computations in constrained number systems.

107. What is a Hamiltonian path and cycle?
Answer: A Hamiltonian path is a path in a graph that visits every vertex exactly once. A Hamiltonian cycle is a Hamiltonian path that starts and ends at the same vertex. Unlike Euler paths, Hamiltonian paths focus on vertices instead of edges. These are important in optimization problems like the traveling salesman problem. Determining their existence is NP-complete, making them central to complexity theory and algorithm design.

108. Explain the concept of logical equivalence with an example.
Answer: Two logical statements are logically equivalent if they yield the same truth value under all possible truth assignments. For example, "$P \rightarrow Q$" is logically equivalent to "$\neg P \vee Q$". Logical equivalence is used in simplifying logical expressions, proving the validity of arguments, and designing logic circuits. It is often proven using truth tables or logical identities. Recognizing equivalent expressions improves efficiency in computation and reasoning.

109. What is a Hasse diagram?
Answer: A Hasse diagram is a graphical representation of a finite partially ordered set (poset) that omits edges implied by transitivity. It is drawn such that if $a < b$, then b is placed higher than a, and an upward edge is drawn from a to b. Hasse diagrams are useful in visualizing order relations, such as divisibility, subset inclusion, and hierarchy structures. They simplify understanding of orderings in lattice theory and algebra.

110. What are the applications of set theory in computer science?
Answer: Set theory is fundamental to computer science. It underlies database operations (e.g., union, intersection), logic programming, formal language theory, and software specifications. It is used in defining data structures like sets, hash sets, and graphs. Concepts like Cartesian products and power sets are used in relational databases and product automata. Set theory also provides a basis for discrete structures, making it essential in algorithm design and verification.

111. Explain the concept of a clique in graph theory.
Answer: A clique in a graph is a subset of vertices such that every pair of vertices is connected by an edge. A complete graph is a clique of all vertices. The largest clique in a graph is called the maximum clique. Finding cliques has applications in social network analysis, bioinformatics, and computational chemistry. However, the clique problem is NP-complete, meaning it is computationally intensive to solve for large graphs.

112. What are prime numbers and how are they used in computer science?
Answer: A prime number is a natural number greater than 1 that has no positive divisors other than 1 and itself. Primes are central to number theory and have significant applications in cryptography (e.g., RSA encryption), hashing algorithms, and pseudorandom number generation. They are also used in primality testing and error detection. Efficient prime generation and factorization are critical to secure digital communication.

113. Describe the power set and its properties.
Answer: The power set of a set S is the set of all subsets of S, including the empty set and S itself. If S has n elements, the power set has 2^n elements. For example, the power set of $\{a, b\}$ is $\{\emptyset, \{a\}, \{b\}, \{a, b\}\}$. Power sets are used in probability, logic, and computing all possible configurations of a system. They help in modeling decision-making, state spaces, and feature subsets.

114. What is a multigraph? How does it differ from a simple graph?
Answer: A multigraph is a graph that allows multiple edges between the same pair of vertices. These multiple edges

are called parallel edges. In contrast, a simple graph does not allow parallel edges or loops. Multigraphs are used in transportation networks, where multiple connections between locations exist, or in circuit design with repeated paths. Understanding multigraphs helps model systems with redundancy and alternative pathways.

115. What is the difference between partial order and total order?
Answer: A partial order is a binary relation that is reflexive, antisymmetric, and transitive but not all elements are comparable. A total order (or linear order) is a partial order in which every pair of elements is comparable. For example, subset inclusion among sets is a partial order, while natural numbers with ≤ form a total order. These concepts are used in sorting algorithms, scheduling tasks, and data hierarchy representation.

116. Explain the difference between directed and undirected graphs.
Answer: In a directed graph, edges have a direction, indicating a one-way relationship between vertices (u → v). In an undirected graph, edges have no direction and indicate a two-way relationship (u — v). Directed graphs are used in modeling tasks with dependencies (e.g., workflows, web links), while undirected graphs are used in social networks and symmetric relationships. The choice depends on the nature of the modeled system.

117. What is a bipartite graph? Provide an example.
Answer: A bipartite graph is a graph whose vertex set can be divided into two disjoint sets such that every edge connects a vertex from one set to the other. There are no edges between vertices of the same set. An example is a job-assignment problem where one set represents people and the other represents jobs. Bipartite graphs are used in matching problems, scheduling, and network flows.

118. What is De Morgan's Law? Explain with example.
Answer: De Morgan's Laws are rules in Boolean algebra and set theory that relate the complement of unions and intersections. The laws state: $\neg(A \land B) = \neg A \lor \neg B$ and $\neg(A \lor B) = \neg A \land \neg B$. For example, if A = "It is raining", and B = "It is cold", then the negation of "It is raining and cold" is "It is not raining or it is not cold". These laws simplify logic expressions and are vital in circuit design and programming.

119. What is a reflexive relation? Provide an example.
Answer: A relation R on a set A is reflexive if for every element a in A, the pair (a, a) is in R. In other words, every element is related to itself. For example, the relation "is equal to" on integers is reflexive since every integer equals itself. Reflexive relations are foundational in defining equivalence relations and in analyzing self-referential systems in logic and mathematics.

120. What are asymptotic notations in discrete mathematics?
Answer: Asymptotic notations describe the limiting behavior of functions and are used in analyzing algorithm complexity. The common notations are Big O (O), Omega (Ω), and Theta (Θ). Big O describes an upper bound, Omega a lower bound, and Theta an exact bound. For example, if an algorithm takes f(n) = 3n^2 + 2n + 1 steps, it is O(n^2). These notations help in comparing algorithm efficiency and scalability.

121. What is the Cartesian product of sets?
Answer: The Cartesian product of two sets A and B, denoted $A \times B$, is the set of all ordered pairs (a, b) where $a \in A$ and $b \in B$. For example, if $A = \{1, 2\}$ and $B = \{x, y\}$, then $A \times B = \{(1, x), (1, y), (2, x), (2, y)\}$. Cartesian products are used in relational databases, coordinate geometry, and formal language theory. They provide a framework for pairing elements and constructing relations.

122. What is a logic gate and how is it related to Boolean algebra?
Answer: A logic gate is an electronic device that performs a basic logical operation on one or more binary inputs and produces a binary output. Logic gates include AND, OR, NOT, NAND, NOR, XOR, and XNOR. These gates implement Boolean algebra operations in digital circuits. Boolean expressions can be translated into combinations of gates, making them essential in circuit design, computing hardware, and digital systems.

123. Explain the concept of a minimal spanning tree.
Answer: A minimal spanning tree (MST) is a spanning tree of a connected, weighted graph that has the minimum

possible total edge weight. MST includes all vertices and avoids cycles. Algorithms like Kruskal's and Prim's are used to find MSTs. Applications include network design (telecom, transportation), clustering, and approximation algorithms. Finding an MST ensures optimal resource usage and connectivity in graph-based systems.

124. What is a function? Define injective, surjective, and bijective functions.
Answer: A function f from set A to set B assigns each element in A to exactly one element in B. A function is injective (one-to-one) if different elements in A map to different elements in B. It is surjective (onto) if every element in B has a pre-image in A. A function is bijective if it is both injective and surjective. Bijective functions have inverses and are essential in mapping and coding.

125. What is the difference between a relation and a function?
Answer: A relation from set A to B is a subset of the Cartesian product A × B and can associate multiple elements of A with elements in B. A function is a special type of relation where each element of A is related to exactly one element in B. All functions are relations, but not all relations are functions. Understanding this distinction is crucial in database design, mapping models, and mathematical reasoning.

126. What is the pigeonhole principle and where is it used?
Answer: The pigeonhole principle states that if more items are placed into fewer containers, then at least one container must hold more than one item. Formally, if n+1n+1n+1 or more items are placed into nnn containers, then at least one container has more than one item. It is widely used in combinatorics, number theory, and computer science to prove the existence of duplicates or repetitions, such as proving that in a group of 13 people, at least two share a birth month.

127. Differentiate between direct and indirect proofs in discrete mathematics.
Answer: A direct proof establishes the truth of a proposition by logically deducing it from known facts or premises using valid reasoning. In contrast, an indirect proof (like proof by contradiction or contrapositive) proves a proposition by showing that assuming the opposite leads to a contradiction. Both methods are essential in mathematics; for example, to prove that the square root of 2 is irrational, an indirect proof is typically used.

128. What is an antichain in partially ordered sets?
Answer: In a partially ordered set (poset), an antichain is a subset in which no two elements are comparable, i.e., for any two elements aaa and bbb in the antichain, neither a≤ba \leq ba≤b nor b≤ab \leq ab≤a holds. Antichains are significant in order theory and are used in applications such as task scheduling and data organization where independence of elements is required.

129. Define a bipartite graph and its applications.
Answer: A bipartite graph is a graph whose vertex set can be divided into two disjoint sets UUU and VVV, such that every edge connects a vertex in UUU to one in VVV, with no edge between vertices in the same set. Bipartite graphs are used in matching problems, job assignments, and network flows. For example, in a job allocation problem, workers and tasks can be represented as separate sets in a bipartite graph.

130. What is the purpose of generating functions in combinatorics?
Answer: Generating functions are algebraic expressions, often power series, that encode sequences and facilitate operations like finding closed-form expressions, solving recurrence relations, and counting combinatorial objects. A generating function for a sequence ana_nan is given by G(x)=∑n=0∞anxnG(x) = \sum_{n=0}^\infty a_n x^nG(x)=∑n=0∞anxn. They are powerful tools in enumerative combinatorics and algorithm analysis.

131. Explain the concept of Hasse diagrams.
Answer: A Hasse diagram is a visual representation of a finite partially ordered set (poset) where elements are represented as vertices and edges indicate the order relation without showing transitive edges. These diagrams simplify the visualization of posets by omitting unnecessary arrows and are widely used in order theory, lattice theory, and database dependency modeling.

132. What is an incidence matrix in graph theory?

Answer: An incidence matrix is a matrix that represents the relationship between vertices and edges in a graph. For a graph with vvv vertices and eee edges, the incidence matrix is a v×ev \times ev×e matrix where the entry is 1 (or -1 for directed graphs) if the vertex is incident to the edge, and 0 otherwise. It provides a compact way to represent sparse graphs and is useful in network analysis and electrical circuit modeling.

133. Describe the difference between injective, surjective, and bijective functions.

Answer: An injective (one-to-one) function maps distinct elements of the domain to distinct elements of the codomain. A surjective (onto) function covers every element of the codomain at least once. A bijective function is both injective and surjective, meaning it forms a perfect pairing between domain and codomain elements. These concepts are essential in understanding function properties, invertibility, and data mapping in computer science.

134. What is an example of a non-distributive lattice?

Answer: A non-distributive lattice is a lattice in which the distributive law does not hold, i.e., a∧(b∨c)≠(a∧b)∨(a∧c)a \land (b \lor c) \neq (a \land b) \lor (a \land c)a∧(b∨c)□=(a∧b)∨(a∧c). A common example is the diamond lattice or the pentagon lattice. These structures arise in algebraic logic and are used to demonstrate the limitations of certain logical frameworks and abstract algebra systems.

135. Explain the role of minimal and maximal elements in a poset.

Answer: In a partially ordered set (poset), a minimal element is one that has no other element less than it, and a maximal element has no other element greater than it. A poset can have multiple minimal or maximal elements. These elements help identify extremal elements in data structures, optimization problems, and scheduling tasks. They are not necessarily the least or greatest elements unless they are comparable to all others in the set.

Chapter 7: Most Asked Questions Part-B

1. What are the properties of binary relations?

Answer: Binary relations have several properties that define their behavior on a set. These include reflexivity (every element relates to itself), symmetry (if a is related to b, then b is related to a), antisymmetry (if both aRb and bRa, then a must equal b), and transitivity (if a is related to b and b is related to c, then a is related to c). A relation may possess one, many, or none of these properties, and understanding them is essential in analyzing structures in discrete mathematics, such as orderings, graphs, and equivalence relations.

2. Explain the pigeonhole principle with an example.

Answer: The pigeonhole principle states that if n items are placed into m containers and $n > m$, then at least one container must hold more than one item. This principle is useful in proving the inevitability of certain outcomes. For example, if 13 people are in a room and there are only 12 months, at least two people must have the same birth month. It is a fundamental concept in combinatorics, used to demonstrate the existence of duplicates or overlaps in various mathematical problems.

3. What is the principle of inclusion and exclusion?

Answer: The principle of inclusion and exclusion is a counting technique used to find the cardinality of the union of multiple sets. It corrects for overcounting by subtracting the sizes of intersections between sets. For two sets A and B, the principle states $|A \cup B| = |A| + |B| - |A \cap B|$. This concept extends to more sets, alternately adding and subtracting intersections of increasing numbers of sets. It is essential in combinatorics for accurate counting, especially when sets have overlapping elements.

4. What are the applications of recurrence relations in computer science?

Answer: Recurrence relations are used to define sequences based on previous terms and are vital in analyzing algorithms, especially those that use divide-and-conquer approaches. For instance, the time complexity of the Merge Sort algorithm is described by the recurrence $T(n) = 2T(n/2) + O(n)$. Recurrence relations also appear in dynamic programming, data structure analysis, and discrete simulations. They help in deriving closed-form expressions for runtime or memory usage, thereby improving algorithm design and understanding.

5. Define equivalence relation with an example.

Answer: An equivalence relation on a set is a binary relation that is reflexive, symmetric, and transitive. For example, consider the relation "is congruent modulo 5" on the set of integers. Two integers a and b are related if $a \equiv b \pmod{5}$. This relation satisfies all three properties: every number is congruent to itself, if $a \equiv b$ then $b \equiv a$, and if $a \equiv b$ and $b \equiv c$ then $a \equiv c$. Equivalence relations partition a set into disjoint equivalence classes, grouping elements with similar characteristics.

6. What is a tautology in propositional logic?

Answer: A tautology is a logical statement that is always true regardless of the truth values of its individual components. In propositional logic, a tautology is a formula that evaluates to true under every possible truth assignment for its propositional variables. For example, the statement P∨¬PP \lor \neg PP∨¬P (law of excluded middle) is a tautology because it is true whether PPP is true or false. Tautologies are significant in logical proofs and theorem validation because they reflect statements that are universally valid. Recognizing tautologies is essential in logic design, mathematics, and computer science.

7. Explain the difference between injective, surjective, and bijective functions.

Answer: In mathematics, these terms describe the nature of functions in terms of mapping between sets. An injective function (one-to-one) maps distinct elements of the domain to distinct elements of the codomain. A surjective function (onto) ensures that every element of the codomain is mapped to by at least one element of the domain. A bijective function is both injective and surjective, meaning every element of the domain maps to a unique and existing element in the codomain, and vice versa. These properties are crucial in defining invertible functions and understanding mappings in discrete mathematics.

8. What is an equivalence relation? Give an example.
Answer: An equivalence relation on a set is a binary relation that satisfies three properties: reflexivity, symmetry, and transitivity. Reflexivity means every element is related to itself; symmetry means if aaa is related to bbb, then bbb is related to aaa; transitivity means if aaa is related to bbb and bbb is related to ccc, then aaa is related to ccc. An example is the relation "has the same remainder when divided by 3" on integers. This relation satisfies all three properties and hence is an equivalence relation. Equivalence relations help partition sets into equivalence classes.

9. Describe the pigeonhole principle with an example.
Answer: The pigeonhole principle states that if nnn items are placed into mmm containers and n>mn > mn>m, then at least one container must contain more than one item. This principle is used in combinatorics and proofs. For example, if there are 13 pairs of socks in a drawer and you pick 14 individual socks randomly, then at least one pair will be matched because there are only 13 types. The pigeonhole principle is a simple yet powerful tool in proving existence results and ensuring repetition under constraints.

10. What is a Hasse diagram?
Answer: A Hasse diagram is a graphical representation of a finite partially ordered set (poset) without showing all the relations explicitly. In a Hasse diagram, elements are represented as vertices, and edges represent the cover relation (directly connected and ordered elements). The diagram omits reflexive and transitive relations for clarity. Elements are arranged vertically so that if a<ba < ba<b, then bbb appears higher than aaa. Hasse diagrams are widely used in lattice theory, hierarchy visualization, and simplification of ordering structures in discrete mathematics.

11. What is a lattice in discrete mathematics?
Answer: A lattice is a special kind of partially ordered set (poset) in which every pair of elements has a unique least upper bound (called join) and greatest lower bound (called meet). The lattice structure is used to represent algebraic systems like Boolean algebras, modular lattices, and distributive lattices. For example, the set of natural numbers with the operations of maximum and minimum forms a lattice. Lattices have wide applications in logic, data mining, and computer science, especially in access control, knowledge representation, and optimization problems.

12. Define a Boolean algebra and state its basic properties.
Answer: A Boolean algebra is a mathematical structure that captures the essence of logic operations. It consists of a set BBB equipped with two binary operations (usually AND $\wedge$ and OR $\vee$), a unary operation (NOT $\neg$), and two distinct elements (0 and 1) such that it satisfies certain axioms: commutativity, associativity, distributivity, identity elements, and complements. Boolean algebras model logic gates and circuits in computer science and are foundational to digital electronics and binary decision-making processes.

13. What is a recurrence relation? Provide an example.
Answer: A recurrence relation is an equation that recursively defines a sequence where each term is a function of its preceding terms. It is widely used in algorithm analysis, particularly in computing the complexity of recursive algorithms. For example, the Fibonacci sequence is defined by F(n)=F(n−1)+F(n−2)F(n) = F(n-1) + F(n-2)F(n)=F(n−1)+F(n−2), with F(0)=0F(0) = 0F(0)=0 and F(1)=1F(1) = 1F(1)=1. Solving recurrence relations helps determine explicit formulas for sequences and plays a key role in dynamic programming and discrete modeling.

14. Explain the principle of mathematical induction.
Answer: Mathematical induction is a proof technique used to prove that a statement holds for all natural numbers. It consists of two steps: the base case, where the statement is verified for the initial value (usually n=0n = 0n=0 or n=1n = 1n=1); and the inductive step, where it is shown that if the statement holds for n=kn = kn=k, then it also holds for n=k+1n = k+1n=k+1. By proving these two steps, the statement is established for all nnn. It is commonly used to validate formulas and algorithm correctness.

15. What is a bipartite graph? How can you check if a graph is bipartite?
Answer: A bipartite graph is a graph whose vertices can be divided into two disjoint sets such that no two vertices within the same set are adjacent. Equivalently, it has no odd-length cycles. To check if a graph is bipartite, you can use Breadth-First Search (BFS) to attempt a 2-coloring: assign colors alternately to neighboring vertices. If no

adjacent vertices share the same color, the graph is bipartite. These graphs are used in matching problems, scheduling, and network modeling.

16. Define Euler's theorem in the context of graph theory.
Answer: Euler's theorem in graph theory states that a connected undirected graph has an Eulerian circuit (a cycle that uses every edge exactly once and starts and ends at the same vertex) if and only if every vertex has an even degree. If exactly two vertices have odd degrees, the graph has an Eulerian path but not an Eulerian circuit. Euler's theorem is fundamental in traversability problems, route planning, and network design, and is named after the mathematician Leonhard Euler.

17. What is a spanning tree? How is it different from a general tree?
Answer: A spanning tree of a connected graph is a subgraph that includes all the vertices of the original graph and is a tree (i.e., connected and acyclic). It has n−1n-1n−1 edges if there are nnn vertices. Unlike a general tree which can be any hierarchical structure, a spanning tree is derived from an existing graph. It is used in designing efficient networks, such as in minimum spanning trees for cost-effective connectivity in communication and transportation systems.

18. Describe the concept of Big-O notation.
Answer: Big-O notation is used to describe the upper bound of an algorithm's running time or space complexity in terms of input size. It provides an asymptotic analysis, helping to compare algorithms independently of hardware or implementation. For example, an algorithm with O(n2)O(n^2)O(n2) complexity will grow quadratically with input size nnn. It simplifies performance evaluation by ignoring constants and lower-order terms. Big-O is vital in algorithm design and complexity theory for evaluating and optimizing computational efficiency.

19. What is the difference between a simple graph and a multigraph?
Answer: A simple graph is an undirected graph that does not contain loops (edges connected at both ends to the same vertex) or multiple edges between the same pair of vertices. A multigraph, on the other hand, allows multiple edges (parallel edges) between the same pair of vertices and may include loops. Simple graphs are widely used in basic theoretical analysis, while multigraphs appear in practical scenarios such as transportation networks and multichannel communication.

20. What is the chromatic number of a graph?
Answer: The chromatic number of a graph is the minimum number of colors needed to color its vertices such that no two adjacent vertices share the same color. It is a key concept in graph coloring, used in scheduling, register allocation in compilers, and frequency assignment in mobile networks. Determining the chromatic number is an NP-Hard problem for general graphs, but known algorithms and heuristics exist for special graph classes.

21. What is a Hamiltonian path and how does it differ from an Eulerian path?
Answer: A Hamiltonian path in a graph is a path that visits each vertex exactly once, whereas an Eulerian path visits every edge exactly once. A Hamiltonian circuit starts and ends at the same vertex and still visits all vertices once. Unlike Eulerian paths, there is no simple criterion for determining whether a Hamiltonian path exists in a general graph. Hamiltonian paths are significant in problems like the traveling salesman problem (TSP), where the goal is to visit every city exactly once with minimal cost.

22. Define partial order and total order. Provide an example for each.
Answer: A partial order is a binary relation that is reflexive, antisymmetric, and transitive. In a partially ordered set (poset), not all elements need to be comparable. For example, the subset relation (⊆) on the power set of a set is a partial order. A total order, on the other hand, is a partial order with comparability: for any two elements aaa and bbb, either a≤ba \leq ba≤b or b≤ab \leq ab≤a holds. An example of total order is the set of natural numbers with the usual ≤ relation.

23. What is the difference between a permutation and a combination?
Answer: Permutation refers to the arrangement of items in a specific order, while combination refers to the selection of items without regard to order. For permutations, order matters—thus, P(n,r)=n!(n−r)!P(n, r) = \frac{n!}{(n -

r)!}P(n,r)=(n−r)!n!, whereas for combinations, order does not matter, so C(n,r)=n!r!(n−r)!C(n, r) = \frac{n!}{r!(n - r)!}C(n,r)=r!(n−r)!n!. For example, the arrangements "ABC" and "CAB" are different permutations but the same combination. These concepts are essential in probability, counting, and discrete optimization.

24. Explain the concept of graph isomorphism.

Answer: Graph isomorphism is a one-to-one correspondence between the vertex sets of two graphs that preserves adjacency. Two graphs GGG and HHH are isomorphic if there exists a bijective function f:V(G)→V(H)f: V(G) \rightarrow V(H)f:V(G)→V(H) such that any two vertices uuu and vvv in GGG are adjacent if and only if f(u)f(u)f(u) and f(v)f(v)f(v) are adjacent in HHH. Isomorphic graphs have the same number of vertices, edges, and degree sequences. Identifying graph isomorphism is useful in chemical structures, database indexing, and pattern recognition.

25. What is a generating function in combinatorics?

Answer: A generating function is a formal power series whose coefficients encode information about a sequence. It is used as a powerful tool in solving recurrence relations, counting problems, and finding closed-form expressions. For a sequence a0,a1,a2,...a_0, a_1, a_2, \dotsa0,a1,a2,..., its generating function is G(x)=a0+a1x+a2x2+...G(x) = a_0 + a_1x + a_2x^2 + \dotsG(x)=a0+a1x+a2x2+.... By manipulating generating functions algebraically, we can extract useful properties of sequences and simplify complex combinatorial problems, especially in partition theory and probability.

26. Define a relation and list its types with examples.

Answer: A relation RRR from set AAA to set BBB is a subset of the Cartesian product A×BA \times BA×B, consisting of ordered pairs (a,b)(a, b)(a,b). Types of relations include:

Reflexive: aRaaRaaRa for all a∈Aa \in Aa∈A (e.g., "equal to" relation).

Symmetric: If aRbaRbaRb, then bRabRabRa (e.g., "is sibling of").

Transitive: If aRbaRbaRb and bRcbRcbRc, then aRcaRcaRc (e.g., "is ancestor of").

Antisymmetric: If aRbaRbaRb and bRabRabRa, then a=ba = ba=b (e.g., "less than or equal to").

Relations are crucial in defining orderings and equivalence in sets.

27. What is the inclusion-exclusion principle?

Answer: The inclusion-exclusion principle is a formula used to count the number of elements in the union of multiple sets, considering overlaps. For two sets, the principle states:

|A∪B|=|A|+|B|−|A∩B||A \cup B| = |A| + |B| - |A \cap B||A∪B|=|A|+|B|−|A∩B|.

For three sets:

|A∪B∪C|=|A|+|B|+|C|−|A∩B|−|B∩C|−|C∩A|+|A∩B∩C||A \cup B \cup C| = |A| + |B| + |C| - |A \cap B| - |B \cap C| - |C \cap A| + |A \cap B \cap C||A∪B∪C|=|A|+|B|+|C|−|A∩B|−|B∩C|−|C∩A|+|A∩B∩C|.

It corrects for overcounting by subtracting intersections. It is widely used in combinatorics and probability.

28. Differentiate between deterministic and non-deterministic finite automata.

Answer: A deterministic finite automaton (DFA) has exactly one transition for each symbol from each state, ensuring a unique computation path. A non-deterministic finite automaton (NFA), however, can have multiple transitions for the same input symbol or even ε-transitions (without consuming input), leading to multiple paths. Despite their differences, NFAs and DFAs recognize the same class of languages—regular languages. However, DFAs are easier to implement, while NFAs are often simpler to construct for theoretical problems.

29. What is the principle of duality in Boolean algebra?

Answer: The principle of duality in Boolean algebra states that every algebraic expression remains valid if we interchange AND (∧) with OR (∨), and 0 with 1 throughout the expression. For example, the dual of the identity a+0=aa + 0 = aa+0=a is a·1=aa \cdot 1 = aa·1=a. This principle is helpful in simplifying Boolean expressions and designing digital logic circuits. It highlights the symmetry inherent in Boolean algebra and provides a method to derive new valid identities from known ones.

30. Define a connected graph and a complete graph.

Answer: A connected graph is a graph where there is a path between every pair of vertices. If any vertex is unreachable, the graph is disconnected. A complete graph is a special type of connected graph where every pair of distinct vertices is connected by a unique edge. A complete graph with nnn vertices has n(n−1)2\frac{n(n-1)}{2}2n(n−1) edges and is denoted as KnK_nKn. Complete graphs are used in network modeling, where maximum connectivity is required.

31. What are independent sets and cliques in graphs?
Answer: An independent set in a graph is a set of vertices with no edges connecting them, meaning no two vertices in the set are adjacent. A clique is the opposite: a subset of vertices in which every pair of vertices is connected by an edge. Finding maximum independent sets and cliques are classic problems in graph theory and are computationally hard (NP-Complete), with applications in social networks, bioinformatics, and optimization.

32. Explain the concept of modular arithmetic with an example.
Answer: Modular arithmetic deals with integers under a wrapping-around system, based on a modulus nnn. In modulo nnn, two integers aaa and bbb are equivalent if they leave the same remainder when divided by nnn, written as a≡b (mod n)a \equiv b \ (\text{mod } n)a≡b (mod n). For example, 17≡5 (mod 12)17 \equiv 5 \ (\text{mod } 12)17≡5 (mod 12). Modular arithmetic is essential in number theory, cryptography, hashing, and clock arithmetic.

33. What is the handshake theorem in graph theory?
Answer: The handshake theorem states that in any undirected graph, the sum of the degrees of all vertices is twice the number of edges. Mathematically, ∑deg(v)=2|E|\sum \deg(v) = 2|E|∑deg(v)=2|E|. This implies that the number of vertices with odd degree must be even. The theorem gets its name from the idea that a handshake involves two people—each edge connects two vertices. It's used in analyzing graph structures and proving basic graph properties.

34. Differentiate between depth-first search and breadth-first search.
Answer: Depth-First Search (DFS) explores as far as possible along a branch before backtracking, using a stack (either explicitly or via recursion). Breadth-First Search (BFS) explores all neighbors of a node before going to the next level, using a queue. DFS is useful in pathfinding, topological sorting, and detecting cycles. BFS is ideal for finding the shortest path in unweighted graphs and level-order traversal. Both algorithms are foundational in graph traversal and AI.

35. What is a directed acyclic graph (DAG)?
Answer: A Directed Acyclic Graph (DAG) is a graph with directed edges and no cycles. This means there is no way to start at a vertex and return to it by following directed edges. DAGs are widely used in modeling processes with dependencies, such as scheduling, task execution orders, and compiler design. One common application is topological sorting, which provides a linear ordering of vertices based on their dependencies.

36. Define cardinality of a set. How do you compare cardinalities?
Answer: The cardinality of a set refers to the number of elements in it. For finite sets, it's simply the count of elements. For infinite sets, we compare cardinalities using one-to-one correspondences. Two sets have the same cardinality if there exists a bijection between them. For example, the set of natural numbers and even numbers both have countably infinite cardinality. Cardinality is essential in set theory and understanding sizes of infinite sets.

37. What is an adjacency matrix and how is it used?
Answer: An adjacency matrix is a square matrix used to represent a graph, where the entry A[i][j]A[i][j]A[i][j] is 1 (or the weight) if there is an edge from vertex iii to vertex jjj, and 0 otherwise. It is used for efficient representation of dense graphs, graph algorithms like path finding, and computing powers of matrices to find reachability. For undirected graphs, the matrix is symmetric. Adjacency matrices allow use of linear algebra in graph processing.

38. Describe the concept of a minimal spanning tree.
Answer: A minimal spanning tree (MST) of a connected, weighted graph is a subgraph that connects all vertices with the minimum total edge weight and no cycles. Algorithms like Kruskal's and Prim's are used to compute MSTs. MSTs are widely used in network design (e.g., minimizing cable length), clustering, and transportation. The MST ensures connectivity with the lowest possible cost.

39. What is the power set of a set? Give an example.
Answer: The power set of a set SSS is the set of all possible subsets of SSS, including the empty set and SSS itself. If SSS has nnn elements, then the power set has 2n2^n2n subsets. For example, if S={a,b}S = \{a, b\}S={a,b}, then the power set is {∅,{a},{b},{a,b}}\{\emptyset, \{a\}, \{b\}, \{a, b\}\}{∅,{a},{b},{a,b}}. Power sets are fundamental in combinatorics and logical analysis.

40. What is the difference between a subset and a proper subset?
Answer: A subset AAA of set BBB is such that every element of AAA is also in BBB, denoted A⊆BA \subseteq BA⊆B. A proper subset is a subset that is not equal to BBB; that is, A⊂BA \subset BA⊂B and A≠BA \neq BA□=B. Every proper subset is a subset, but not vice versa. Understanding subsets is crucial in logic, set theory, and defining hierarchical structures.

41. What is a spanning tree? Explain its properties.
Answer: A spanning tree of a graph is a subgraph that includes all the vertices of the original graph connected by the minimum number of edges such that there are no cycles. Essentially, it is a tree that spans all the vertices. For a graph with `n` vertices, a spanning tree contains exactly `n-1` edges. Properties of a spanning tree include connectivity (all nodes are reachable), acyclicity (no cycles are present), and minimalism (no extra edges). Spanning trees are useful in network design, like laying cables using the least amount of wire while ensuring connectivity.

42. What is a planar graph? Provide examples.
Answer: A planar graph is a graph that can be drawn on a plane without any of its edges crossing. In other words, its edges intersect only at their endpoints. A classic example is a triangle or square with diagonals excluded. The famous Kuratowski's theorem provides a test for planarity: a graph is non-planar if it contains a subgraph that is a subdivision of either K_5 (complete graph of five vertices) or $K_{3,3}$ (complete bipartite graph). Planar graphs are significant in circuit design, geography, and computer graphics.

43. What is the principle of duality in set theory?
Answer: The principle of duality in set theory states that every algebraic expression or identity involving the set operations union (∪), intersection (∩), universal set (U), and empty set (∅) remains valid if we systematically replace ∪ with ∩, ∩ with ∪, U with ∅, and ∅ with U. This principle helps in deriving dual expressions and verifying the validity of identities. For instance, the dual of $A \cup \emptyset = A$ is $A \cap U = A$. It provides a symmetric structure to set identities and logical expressions.

44. What are multigraphs and pseudographs?
Answer: A multigraph is a graph that allows multiple edges (parallel edges) between the same set of vertices. A pseudograph extends this concept further by allowing not only multiple edges but also loops—edges that connect a vertex to itself. These types of graphs are used to model real-world situations where multiple relationships or connections exist between entities, such as transportation systems with multiple routes between cities or self-loops in social networks indicating self-referencing actions.

45. Explain the concept of finite and infinite sets with examples.
Answer: A set is finite if it contains a limited number of elements, whereas it is infinite if the number of elements cannot be counted or is unbounded. For example, the set of days in a week {Monday, Tuesday, ..., Sunday} is finite as it has 7 elements. On the other hand, the set of all natural numbers {1, 2, 3, ...} is infinite because there is no end. In discrete mathematics, distinguishing between these two is vital in understanding cardinality, computability, and algorithm complexity.

46. What is the Cartesian product of two sets? Give an example.
Answer: The Cartesian product of two sets A and B, denoted as $A \times B$, is the set of all ordered pairs (a, b) where $a \in A$ and $b \in B$. For example, if $A = \{1, 2\}$ and $B = \{x, y\}$, then $A \times B = \{(1, x), (1, y), (2, x), (2, y)\}$. Cartesian products are foundational in defining relations and functions and are used in database systems, coordinate geometry, and formal logic.

47. What is a lattice in discrete mathematics?
Answer: A lattice is an algebraic structure consisting of a partially ordered set (poset) in which every pair of elements has both a least upper bound (join) and a greatest lower bound (meet). In other words, for any two elements a and b in a lattice, both $a \vee b$ and $a \wedge b$ exist. Lattices are used in order theory, data classification, and formal concept analysis. A common example is the set of all subsets of a set with union and intersection as the join and meet operations.

48. Define the concept of a loop invariant and its role in algorithm design.
Answer: A loop invariant is a condition that holds true before and after each iteration of a loop during the execution of an algorithm. It is used in proving the correctness of algorithms, particularly iterative ones. The loop invariant helps ensure that the algorithm maintains certain properties throughout its execution and reaches the correct result upon termination. For example, in insertion sort, a loop invariant is that the sub-array before the current index is always sorted.

49. Explain the term 'bijection' and its significance in discrete math.
Answer: A bijection is a function that is both injective (one-to-one) and surjective (onto). This means every element in the domain maps to a unique element in the codomain, and every element in the codomain is the image of exactly one element in the domain. Bijections are important in counting (combinatorics), proving two sets have equal cardinality, and establishing invertible functions. For instance, the mapping $f(x) = x + 1$ from set {1, 2, 3} to {2, 3, 4} is a bijection.

50. What is the significance of truth tables in logic?
Answer: Truth tables are tools used to determine the validity of logical expressions by listing all possible truth values of their variables and the resulting output of the expressions. They are essential in propositional logic for analyzing statements, proving tautologies, contradictions, and logical equivalences. Truth tables are also crucial in digital logic design, where they help derive Boolean functions and understand circuit behavior. For instance, the truth table for the logical AND operation shows the result is true only when both inputs are true.

51. What is the difference between a relation and a function in discrete mathematics?
Answer: A **relation** from set A to set B is any subset of the Cartesian product $A \times B$, meaning it can associate one or more elements of A to one or more elements of B. A **function**, however, is a special type of relation where each element in set A is associated with exactly one element in set B. For example, a relation may contain (1, 2), (1, 3), but a function cannot. Functions are a more constrained concept and are vital in algorithm design, database queries, and modeling mathematical structures.

52. What are equivalence relations? Give an example.
Answer: An **equivalence relation** on a set is a relation that is **reflexive**, **symmetric**, and **transitive**. These properties ensure that the elements are related in a way similar to equality. For instance, the relation "congruent modulo n" on integers is an equivalence relation: if $a \equiv b \bmod n$, then it's reflexive ($a \equiv a$), symmetric (if $a \equiv b$ then $b \equiv a$), and transitive (if $a \equiv b$ and $b \equiv c$, then $a \equiv c$). Equivalence relations partition sets into equivalence classes, useful in simplifying data and logical analysis.

53. Define partial order relation and give its characteristics.
Answer: A **partial order relation** on a set is a relation that is **reflexive**, **antisymmetric**, and **transitive**. It allows the elements to be arranged in a certain order but not necessarily every pair is comparable. A good example is the "subset" relation $\subseteq$ among sets. Not all subsets are directly comparable ($A \subseteq B$ or $B \subseteq A$), hence it's only a *partial* order. Partial orders are foundational in hierarchy modeling, scheduling, and dependency resolution.

54. What is a Boolean algebra?
Answer: A **Boolean algebra** is a mathematical structure that captures the logic of binary variables and operations. It includes a set with two binary operations (usually AND $\wedge$, OR $\vee$) and one unary operation (NOT $\neg$), along with identity and complement elements. Boolean algebra is fundamental in digital logic design, switching circuits, and theoretical computer science. It satisfies properties like commutativity, associativity, distributivity, identity, complement, and De Morgan's laws.

55. What are De Morgan's laws in logic and set theory?

Answer: **De Morgan's Laws** describe how logical operations and set operations relate under negation. In logic:

$\neg(P \wedge Q) \equiv \neg P \vee \neg Q$

$\neg(P \vee Q) \equiv \neg P \wedge \neg Q$

In set theory:

$(A \cap B)' = A' \cup B'$

$(A \cup B)' = A' \cap B'$

These laws are crucial in simplifying logical expressions and are widely used in programming, circuit design, and proof strategies.

56. What is the pigeonhole principle?

Answer: The **Pigeonhole Principle** states that if n items are put into m containers and $n > m$, then at least one container must hold more than one item. It's a basic but powerful concept in combinatorics used to prove the existence of repetitions or guarantees. For example, if 13 people are placed in 12 rooms, at least one room must contain more than one person. It's applied in data analysis, cryptography, and proof construction.

57. Explain the principle of inclusion and exclusion.

Answer: The **Principle of Inclusion and Exclusion** is used in combinatorics to count the number of elements in the union of multiple sets, especially when they overlap. For two sets A and B:

$|A \cup B| = |A| + |B| - |A \cap B|$

For three sets A, B, C:

$|A \cup B \cup C| = |A| + |B| + |C| - |A \cap B| - |A \cap C| - |B \cap C| + |A \cap B \cap C|$

This principle helps in solving problems involving overlapping categories.

58. What is the difference between a simple graph and a complete graph?

Answer: A **simple graph** is an undirected graph without loops or multiple edges between the same pair of vertices. A **complete graph** is a simple graph in which every pair of distinct vertices is connected by a unique edge. For example, a complete graph with 4 vertices (K_4) has 6 edges. Simple graphs can represent minimal connections, while complete graphs depict maximum connectivity. These concepts are critical in networking, communication, and graph theory.

59. What are bipartite graphs? How can we identify them?

Answer: A **bipartite graph** is a graph whose vertices can be divided into two disjoint sets such that no two vertices within the same set are adjacent. Formally, all edges must go between the two sets. A classic way to check if a graph is bipartite is through **graph coloring**: if it is 2-colorable (no two adjacent vertices have the same color), then it is bipartite. Bipartite graphs are used in matchmaking algorithms, job assignments, and scheduling.

60. What is a power set? Give an example.

Answer: A **power set** is the set of all subsets of a given set, including the empty set and the set itself. If a set has n elements, its power set has 2^n subsets. For example, for set A = {1, 2}, the power set is P(A) = {∅, {1}, {2}, {1,2}}. Power sets are important in combinatorics, logic, and theoretical computer science where all possible combinations of elements need to be considered.

61. What is the difference between a simple graph and a multigraph?

Answer: A simple graph is an unweighted, undirected graph that has no loops (edges connected at both ends to the same vertex) and no more than one edge between any two different vertices. In contrast, a multigraph may have multiple edges (parallel edges) between the same pair of vertices and may include loops. Multigraphs are useful in modeling scenarios where multiple relationships can exist between entities, such as in transportation or communication networks.

62. Define chromatic number in graph theory and its significance.
Answer: The chromatic number of a graph is the minimum number of colors needed to color its vertices so that no two adjacent vertices share the same color. It is an important concept in graph coloring problems and has applications in scheduling, register allocation in compilers, and frequency assignment in mobile networks. Determining the chromatic number is computationally challenging for arbitrary graphs.

63. What is an Eulerian path and how does it differ from a Hamiltonian path?
Answer: An Eulerian path in a graph is a path that traverses every edge exactly once. In contrast, a Hamiltonian path visits every vertex exactly once. A graph has an Eulerian path if it has exactly zero or two vertices of odd degree. Eulerian paths are used in problems like route planning and DNA sequencing, whereas Hamiltonian paths are more related to covering all nodes efficiently.

64. What is a truth table and how is it used in logic?
Answer: A truth table is a tabular representation that lists all possible truth values of a logical expression based on the truth values of its variables. It is used to determine whether a proposition is a tautology, contradiction, or contingency. Truth tables are foundational in digital circuit design, Boolean algebra, and logical proof construction.

65. Define a partially ordered set (poset) and give an example.
Answer: A partially ordered set (poset) is a set equipped with a binary relation that is reflexive, antisymmetric, and transitive. For example, the set of natural numbers with the usual "less than or equal to" ($\leq$) relation forms a poset. Posets are used in scheduling, lattice theory, and hierarchical modeling.

66. Explain the concept of lattice in discrete mathematics.
Answer: A lattice is a special type of poset in which any two elements have a unique least upper bound (join) and greatest lower bound (meet). Lattices are used in algebra, logic, and computer science to model hierarchical structures and abstract data types. Boolean algebra itself is a type of lattice.

67. What is a recurrence relation? Provide an example.
Answer: A recurrence relation is an equation that defines a sequence where each term is a function of one or more previous terms. For example, the Fibonacci sequence is defined by the recurrence relation $F(n) = F(n-1) + F(n-2)$, with initial conditions $F(0) = 0$ and $F(1) = 1$. Recurrence relations are widely used in algorithm analysis and dynamic programming.

68. Differentiate between deterministic and non-deterministic algorithms.
Answer: A deterministic algorithm produces the same output for a given input every time it is executed and follows a specific sequence of steps. In contrast, a non-deterministic algorithm can have multiple outcomes for the same input due to choices made during execution. Non-determinism is theoretical in nature and helps in understanding problem complexity, such as NP-completeness.

69. What is a generating function in combinatorics?
Answer: A generating function is a formal power series in which the coefficients represent terms of a sequence. It is a powerful tool used in solving recurrence relations, counting problems, and in analyzing sequences. For example, the generating function for the sequence of natural numbers 1, 2, 3,... is $G(x) = x / (1-x)^2$.

70. What is the principle of mathematical induction?
Answer: Mathematical induction is a proof technique used to prove that a statement holds for all natural numbers. It involves two steps: the base case, where the statement is shown to be true for the initial value (usually $n=1$), and the inductive step, where it is shown that if the statement holds for some k, then it also holds for $k+1$. This method is widely used in proving formulas and properties of sequences.

71. What is a surjective function? Give an example.
Answer: A surjective (onto) function is one where every element in the codomain is the image of at least one element from the domain. For example, the function $f(x) = 2x$ from the set of integers to even integers is surjective.

Surjective functions ensure complete coverage of the target set and are fundamental in function analysis and transformations.

72. Define bijective function and its properties.
Answer: A bijective function is both injective (one-to-one) and surjective (onto), meaning every element in the domain maps to a unique element in the codomain, and every element in the codomain is covered. Bijective functions are invertible and form the basis for establishing equivalences between sets, especially in counting and set theory.

73. What is the role of adjacency matrices in graph representation?
Answer: An adjacency matrix is a 2D array used to represent a graph, where the element at row i and column j indicates the presence (and possibly the weight) of an edge between vertices i and j. This representation is useful for dense graphs and allows efficient computation of paths, connectivity, and matrix-based algorithms like Floyd-Warshall.

74. What are combinatorial identities? Provide an example.
Answer: Combinatorial identities are algebraic expressions that equate two different combinatorial expressions. They are used to simplify counting problems. An example is the identity:
$C(n, r) = C(n-1, r) + C(n-1, r-1)$,
which is used in Pascal's triangle and in calculating binomial coefficients.

75. What is the role of propositional logic in computer science?
Answer: Propositional logic provides a framework for designing and analyzing logical statements and reasoning. It is used in programming, algorithms, circuit design, and artificial intelligence. It helps in verifying software correctness, building logic gates, and creating rule-based systems.

76. Define the concept of modular arithmetic.
Answer: Modular arithmetic deals with integers wrapped around after reaching a certain value called the modulus. For example, in mod 5 arithmetic, $7 \equiv 2 \pmod{5}$. It is fundamental in number theory, cryptography (e.g., RSA algorithm), hashing functions, and computer algorithms.

77. What is the difference between a subset and a proper subset?
Answer: A subset A of a set B contains only elements that are also in B. A proper subset is a subset that is not equal to the original set, i.e., $A \subset B$ but $A \neq B$. The distinction is important in set theory and is used in operations involving combinations, logic, and data structures.

78. Explain De Morgan's Laws with examples.
Answer: De Morgan's Laws provide rules for negating logical expressions:
$\neg(P \land Q) \equiv (\neg P \lor \neg Q)$ and
$\neg(P \lor Q) \equiv (\neg P \land \neg Q)$.
These laws are essential in simplifying logical expressions and are used extensively in programming, digital logic design, and formal proofs.

79. What is the difference between countable and uncountable sets?
Answer: A set is countable if its elements can be listed in a sequence (i.e., it has the same cardinality as the natural numbers). Examples include the integers and rational numbers. An uncountable set, like the real numbers, cannot be listed in such a manner. This distinction is important in set theory and helps define different sizes of infinity.

80. Define a contradiction in logic with an example.
Answer: A contradiction is a logical statement that is always false, regardless of the truth values of its components. For example, the statement "$P \land \neg P$" (P and not P) is a contradiction. Contradictions are used in proof by contradiction, where assuming the negation of a proposition leads to a contradiction, thus proving the original proposition true.

81. What is the pigeonhole principle and how is it applied?
Answer: The pigeonhole principle states that if more items are put into fewer containers, then at least one container must hold more than one item. Mathematically, if nnn items are placed in mmm containers and n>mn > mn>m, then at least one container has more than one item. This principle is used in combinatorics, probability, and computer science to prove the existence of certain conditions, such as hash collisions, repeated elements, or unavoidable overlaps.

82. Explain the difference between a tautology and a contradiction.
Answer: A tautology is a logical statement that is always true, regardless of the truth values of its variables (e.g., P∨¬PP \lor \neg PP∨¬P). A contradiction is always false (e.g., P∧¬PP \land \neg PP∧¬P). Tautologies are used to validate logical arguments, while contradictions help identify inconsistencies or perform indirect proofs like proof by contradiction.

83. What is an isomorphism in graph theory?
Answer: An isomorphism in graph theory is a one-to-one correspondence between the vertices and edges of two graphs such that the adjacency is preserved. Two graphs are isomorphic if they have the same structure but possibly different labels. Graph isomorphism is important in pattern recognition, chemical compound modeling, and network analysis.

84. Define reflexive, symmetric, and transitive relations with examples.
Answer:
A relation is **reflexive** if every element is related to itself (e.g., aRaaRaaRa).
Symmetric if aRbaRbaRb implies bRabRabRa.
Transitive if aRbaRbaRb and bRcbRcbRc imply aRcaRcaRc.
For example, in the relation "is equal to" on integers: it's reflexive (5 = 5), symmetric (if 5 = 7, then 7 = 5), and transitive (if 5 = 7 and 7 = 9, then 5 = 9).

85. What is a minimal spanning tree and where is it used?
Answer: A minimal spanning tree (MST) is a subset of the edges of a connected, weighted graph that connects all vertices with the minimum possible total edge weight and without forming any cycle. Algorithms like Prim's and Kruskal's are used to find MSTs. MSTs are used in network design (e.g., telecommunications, computer networks), road construction, and clustering.

86. What is a logical implication and how is it used in proofs?
Answer: A logical implication is a statement of the form "if P, then Q" (denoted P→QP \rightarrow QP→Q). It is true in all cases except when P is true and Q is false. Implications are essential in logical reasoning and proof techniques, such as direct proof, contraposition, and mathematical induction.

87. What is a power set? Give an example.
Answer: A power set is the set of all subsets of a given set, including the empty set and the set itself. If a set has nnn elements, its power set has 2n2^n2n elements. For example, the power set of {a,b}\{a, b\}{a,b} is {∅,{a},{b},{a,b}}\{\emptyset, \{a\}, \{b\}, \{a, b\}\}{∅,{a},{b},{a,b}}. Power sets are important in set theory, logic, and combinatorics.

88. What are permutations and how are they different from combinations?
Answer: Permutations are arrangements of items where order matters, while combinations are selections where order does not matter. For example, selecting 2 items from {A, B, C}:
Permutations: AB, AC, BA, BC, CA, CB (6 total).
Combinations: AB, AC, BC (3 total).
Permutations are used in ranking, password generation, and scheduling.

89. Explain the concept of binary trees and their applications.
Answer: A binary tree is a hierarchical data structure where each node has at most two children, commonly referred

to as the left and right child. Binary trees are used in various applications such as binary search trees (for fast lookup), expression trees (in compilers), and Huffman coding trees (in data compression).

90. What is the difference between DFS and BFS traversal in graphs?
Answer: Depth-First Search (DFS) explores as far as possible along each branch before backtracking, using a stack or recursion. Breadth-First Search (BFS) explores all neighbors at the current depth before moving to the next level, using a queue. DFS is useful for pathfinding and topological sorting, while BFS is ideal for finding the shortest path in unweighted graphs.

91. What is the inclusion-exclusion principle in set theory?
Answer: The inclusion-exclusion principle is used to count the number of elements in the union of overlapping sets. For two sets A and B:
|A∪B|=|A|+|B|−|A∩B||A \cup B| = |A| + |B| - |A \cap B||A∪B|=|A|+|B|−|A∩B|
It corrects the overcounting of shared elements and extends to three or more sets. It's widely used in probability, counting problems, and Venn diagram analysis.

92. Define the term algorithm and its characteristics.
Answer: An algorithm is a finite, well-defined sequence of steps to solve a problem or perform a computation. Key characteristics include:

Input (zero or more inputs),
Output (at least one output),
Finiteness (terminates in finite steps),
Definiteness (clear and unambiguous steps),
Effectiveness (each step is basic and feasible).
Algorithms are central in computer science, used in sorting, searching, and optimization.

93. What is a finite state machine and its types?
Answer: A finite state machine (FSM) is a computational model consisting of a finite number of states, transitions, inputs, and outputs. It is used to model sequential logic and behavior. There are two main types:
Deterministic FSM (DFA): Exactly one transition per input.
Non-deterministic FSM (NFA): Can have multiple transitions per input.
FSMs are used in text processing, compilers, and control systems.

94. What are logic gates and their types?
Answer: Logic gates are basic building blocks of digital circuits that implement Boolean functions. Common types include:
AND, OR, NOT
NAND, NOR, XOR, XNOR
Each gate takes one or more binary inputs and produces a binary output. They are used in arithmetic circuits, memory, and processors.

95. What is a directed acyclic graph (DAG) and where is it used?
Answer: A Directed Acyclic Graph (DAG) is a graph with directed edges and no cycles. DAGs are used in modeling tasks with dependencies, such as scheduling, data processing pipelines, and version control systems. In computer science, they are also used in representing expressions, course prerequisites, and workflows.

96. What is the binomial theorem and its application?
Answer: The binomial theorem gives the expansion of powers of a binomial expression:
(a+b)n=∑k=0n(nk)an−kbk(a + b)^n = \sum_{k=0}^{n} \binom{n}{k} a^{n-k}b^k(a+b)n=∑k=0n(kn)an−kbk
It is used in algebra, probability, and combinatorics for simplifying expressions, calculating coefficients, and solving polynomial problems.

97. What is a Boolean algebra and its importance?
Answer: Boolean algebra is a mathematical structure that deals with binary variables and logical operations. It uses operations like AND, OR, and NOT and follows specific laws (e.g., commutative, associative). It is fundamental in digital electronics, logic design, and computer programming for building and simplifying logical circuits.

98. Define an injective function with an example.
Answer: An injective (one-to-one) function maps each element of the domain to a unique element in the codomain. No two inputs map to the same output. Example: f(x)=2x+1f(x) = 2x + 1f(x)=2x+1 is injective over the set of real numbers. Injectivity ensures distinctiveness in mapping and is crucial in database indexing and functional analysis.

99. What is the principle of duality in Boolean algebra?
Answer: The principle of duality in Boolean algebra states that every algebraic expression remains valid if we interchange AND with OR and 0 with 1 throughout the expression. It helps in deriving dual expressions and understanding logical symmetry. For example, the dual of A+0=AA + 0 = AA+0=A is A·1=AA \cdot 1 = AA·1=A.

100. What are equivalence relations and how are they characterized?
Answer: An equivalence relation on a set is a relation that is reflexive, symmetric, and transitive. It partitions the set into disjoint equivalence classes where every element is equivalent to others in its class. Equivalence relations are used in modular arithmetic, classification problems, and data grouping based on similarity.

101. What is the difference between a function and a relation in discrete mathematics?
Answer: A relation is a set of ordered pairs representing associations between elements of two sets, while a function is a specific type of relation in which each element of the domain is related to exactly one element of the codomain. All functions are relations, but not all relations are functions. For example, the relation {(1,2), (1,3)} is not a function because the input 1 maps to two outputs. Functions must satisfy the uniqueness condition, whereas general relations do not.

102. Explain the term 'power set' with an example.
Answer: The power set of a set is the set of all possible subsets, including the empty set and the set itself. If a set has nnn elements, its power set contains 2n2^n2n subsets. For example, if A={1,2}A = \{1, 2\}A={1,2}, then the power set P(A)={∅,{1},{2},{1,2}}P(A) = \{\emptyset, \{1\}, \{2\}, \{1, 2\}\}P(A)={∅,{1},{2},{1,2}}. Power sets are essential in logic, set theory, and combinatorics.

103. Define the principle of mathematical induction.
Answer: Mathematical induction is a proof technique used to prove that a statement holds for all natural numbers. It involves two steps: the base case and the inductive step. In the base case, we verify the statement for the initial value (usually n=1n = 1n=1). In the inductive step, we assume the statement holds for n=kn = kn=k and prove it holds for n=k+1n = k + 1n=k+1. This method is fundamental in proving properties of sequences and recursive definitions.

104. What is the difference between injective, surjective, and bijective functions?
Answer: An injective function (one-to-one) maps distinct elements of the domain to distinct elements of the codomain. A surjective function (onto) covers every element of the codomain at least once. A bijective function is both injective and surjective, meaning every element of the domain maps to a unique element of the codomain, and every codomain element is used. Bijective functions have inverses, which makes them crucial in set theory and algebra.

105. Describe Hasse diagrams and their significance.
Answer: A Hasse diagram is a graphical representation of a partially ordered set (poset), showing the order relation among elements without redundancy. It omits transitive edges and typically places lower elements at the bottom. Hasse diagrams help visualize hierarchical structures like divisibility among integers or subset relations among sets, making them valuable tools in order theory and lattice theory.

106. What is the difference between a tautology and a contradiction?
Answer: A tautology is a compound statement that is always true regardless of the truth values of its individual

components. A contradiction is a statement that is always false. For example, P∨¬PP \lor \neg PP∨¬P is a tautology, while P∧¬PP \land \neg PP∧¬P is a contradiction. These concepts are central in logic, as they help determine the validity of arguments.

107. Explain the concept of a Boolean function with example.

Answer: A Boolean function is a function that takes binary inputs (0 or 1) and returns binary outputs. It can be represented using truth tables or Boolean expressions. For example, the function f(x,y)=x∧yf(x, y) = x \land yf(x,y)=x∧y returns 1 only when both xxx and yyy are 1. Boolean functions are widely used in digital logic design and computer science.

108. What is the pigeonhole principle and how is it applied?

Answer: The pigeonhole principle states that if more items are placed into fewer containers, then at least one container must hold more than one item. Formally, if nnn items are placed into mmm containers and n>mn > mn>m, at least one container contains more than one item. It is used in combinatorics to prove existence results, such as finding duplicates in a list.

109. Define the concept of poset and its properties.

Answer: A poset (partially ordered set) is a set equipped with a binary relation that is reflexive, antisymmetric, and transitive. It models scenarios where not all elements are comparable. For example, the subset relation ⊆\subseteq⊆ on a power set forms a poset. Posets are fundamental in order theory, lattice theory, and hierarchy representations.

110. What is a recursive function and how is it defined?

Answer: A recursive function is a function that is defined in terms of itself, typically with a base case and a rule for reducing larger inputs. For example, the factorial function f(n)=n·f(n−1)f(n) = n \cdot f(n-1)f(n)=n·f(n−1), with f(0)=1f(0) = 1f(0)=1, is recursive. Recursion is a powerful technique in mathematics and computer science for solving complex problems by breaking them into simpler subproblems.

111. What is the difference between finite and infinite sets with examples?

Answer: A finite set has a countable number of elements that can be listed or measured, while an infinite set has unlimited or uncountable elements. For example, the set A={1,2,3}A = \{1, 2, 3\}A={1,2,3} is finite, as it contains only three elements. On the other hand, the set of natural numbers N={1,2,3,...}\mathbb{N} = \{1, 2, 3, \ldots\}N={1,2,3,...} is infinite because it goes on forever. Understanding this difference is fundamental in set theory, cardinality, and theoretical computer science.

112. Explain the properties of an equivalence relation.

Answer: An equivalence relation is a relation on a set that satisfies three key properties: reflexivity (every element is related to itself), symmetry (if aaa is related to bbb, then bbb is related to aaa), and transitivity (if aaa is related to bbb and bbb to ccc, then aaa is related to ccc). Equivalence relations partition a set into disjoint subsets called equivalence classes, which are essential in grouping elements with similar properties.

113. What is the purpose of the inclusion-exclusion principle?

Answer: The inclusion-exclusion principle is used in combinatorics to calculate the cardinality of the union of multiple sets by including and excluding overlapping elements. For two sets, it is expressed as |A∪B|=|A|+|B|−|A∩B||A \cup B| = |A| + |B| - |A \cap B||A∪B|=|A|+|B|−|A∩B|. This principle helps avoid overcounting and is crucial in problems involving counting elements that belong to one or more sets.

114. Define a semigroup and its properties.

Answer: A semigroup is an algebraic structure consisting of a non-empty set equipped with an associative binary operation. That is, for all a,b,ca, b, ca,b,c in the set, (a∗b)∗c=a∗(b∗c)(a * b) * c = a * (b * c)(a∗b)∗c=a∗(b∗c). Semigroups do not require identity elements or inverses, unlike groups. They are used in automata theory, formal languages, and abstract algebra.

115. What is the difference between a graph and a multigraph?

Answer: A graph is a collection of vertices connected by edges, where each pair of vertices has at most one edge between them. A multigraph allows multiple edges (parallel edges) between the same pair of vertices. Multigraphs are useful in modeling real-world networks like transportation or communication systems where multiple connections can exist between nodes.

116. Explain the concept of chromatic number in graph theory.
Answer: The chromatic number of a graph is the minimum number of colors required to color its vertices so that no two adjacent vertices share the same color. It is a measure of a graph's complexity and is used in problems like scheduling, register allocation, and map coloring. Determining the chromatic number is often a challenging problem in combinatorial optimization.

117. What is the role of adjacency matrices in graph representation?
Answer: An adjacency matrix is a square matrix used to represent a finite graph. The element aija_{ij}aij is 1 if there is an edge from vertex iii to vertex jjj, and 0 otherwise (or the weight in weighted graphs). It provides a convenient way to store and manipulate graph data, especially for dense graphs, and is widely used in algorithms involving graph traversal and pathfinding.

118. Define the term 'logical equivalence' in propositional logic.
Answer: Two logical statements are logically equivalent if they have the same truth values under all possible truth assignments. Logical equivalence is denoted by ≡\equiv≡. For example, P→QP \rightarrow QP→Q is logically equivalent to ¬P∨Q\neg P \lor Q¬P∨Q. Logical equivalences are essential in simplifying expressions and proving the validity of arguments in logic.

119. What is a spanning tree? How is it different from a regular tree?
Answer: A spanning tree of a graph is a subgraph that includes all the vertices of the original graph and is a tree (connected and acyclic). Unlike a regular tree, which may be any tree structure, a spanning tree is derived from an existing graph and connects all its vertices with the minimum number of edges. It is used in network design, optimization, and algorithmic problems like Kruskal's and Prim's algorithms.

120. Explain Euler's formula for planar graphs.
Answer: Euler's formula for planar graphs states that for any connected planar graph, the relationship V−E+F=2V - E + F = 2V−E+F=2 holds, where VVV is the number of vertices, EEE is the number of edges, and FFF is the number of faces (including the outer face). This formula is fundamental in graph theory and topology, helping verify graph planarity and understand surface structures.

121. What is the difference between an isomorphism and homomorphism in graphs?
Answer: An isomorphism is a bijective mapping between two graphs that preserves the structure (edges and vertices), meaning the graphs are structurally identical. A homomorphism is a mapping that preserves edge connectivity but not necessarily bijectively. While isomorphic graphs are indistinguishable in terms of graph theory, homomorphic graphs may differ but maintain some structural similarities. These concepts are crucial in graph matching and network comparison.

122. Describe the principle of duality in Boolean algebra.
Answer: The principle of duality in Boolean algebra states that every algebraic expression remains valid if we swap AND (·) with OR (+) and swap 0 with 1. For example, the dual of A+0=AA + 0 = AA+0=A is A·1=AA \cdot 1 = AA·1=A. Duality allows for concise derivations of new expressions from known theorems and highlights the symmetrical nature of Boolean operations.

123. What is the difference between reflexive and irreflexive relations?
Answer: A relation RRR on a set is reflexive if every element is related to itself, i.e., (a,a)∈R(a, a) \in R(a,a)∈R for all aaa. It is irreflexive if no element is related to itself, i.e., (a,a)∉R(a, a) \notin R(a,a)∈/R for all aaa. Reflexivity is a key property in defining equivalence relations, while irreflexivity is often found in strict orderings like the "less than" relation.

124. What are De Morgan's laws and how are they applied?
Answer: De Morgan's laws are fundamental rules in logic and set theory that relate conjunctions and disjunctions through negation. The laws state:
¬(P∧Q)≡¬P∨¬Q\neg(P \land Q) \equiv \neg P \lor \neg Q¬(P∧Q)≡¬P∨¬Q
¬(P∨Q)≡¬P∧¬Q\neg(P \lor Q) \equiv \neg P \land \neg Q¬(P∨Q)≡¬P∧¬Q
These laws are used to simplify logical expressions and are vital in programming, digital circuit design, and mathematical reasoning.

125. Explain the concept of well-ordered sets.
Answer: A well-ordered set is a totally ordered set in which every non-empty subset has a least element. This concept is significant in number theory and proofs involving transfinite induction. For example, the set of natural numbers N\mathbb{N}N is well-ordered, since every subset of N\mathbb{N}N has a smallest number. Well-ordered sets are foundational in defining ordinal numbers and advanced logic structures.

126. What is an adjacency matrix in graph theory and how is it used?
Answer: An adjacency matrix is a square matrix used to represent a finite graph. The elements of the matrix indicate whether pairs of vertices are adjacent or not in the graph. For a graph with nnn vertices, the matrix is n×nn \times nn×n, where the entry at row iii and column jjj is 1 if there is an edge between vertex iii and vertex jjj, and 0 otherwise. In weighted graphs, the entry may represent the weight of the edge. It is useful for algorithms like Dijkstra's and in checking connectivity and cycles.

127. Explain the concept of a tautology in propositional logic with an example.
Answer: A tautology is a propositional formula that is always true, regardless of the truth values of its individual components. For example, the statement P∨¬PP \lor \neg PP∨¬P (either P is true or not true) is a tautology because it holds under all truth assignments. Tautologies are essential in logical reasoning and are used to validate arguments and construct proofs in discrete mathematics and computer science.

128. Define Euler's formula for planar graphs and its significance.
Answer: Euler's formula for planar graphs states that for any connected planar graph, the relationship between vertices (V), edges (E), and faces (F) is given by V−E+F=2V - E + F = 2V−E+F=2. This formula helps verify if a graph is planar and is instrumental in graph drawing, mesh generation, and geographical mapping systems. It also supports proofs related to the coloring of maps and surfaces.

129. What is the difference between a multigraph and a simple graph?
Answer: A simple graph is an undirected graph that does not contain multiple edges between the same pair of vertices or self-loops. In contrast, a multigraph allows multiple edges (parallel edges) between the same vertices and may include loops (edges connecting a vertex to itself). Multigraphs are used in transportation networks, communication modeling, and systems that allow multiple types of connections between entities.

130. What is a characteristic function in set theory and its application?
Answer: A characteristic function (or indicator function) of a set AAA defined on a universal set UUU is a function χA:U→{0,1}\chi_A: U \rightarrow \{0,1\}χA:U→{0,1}, where χA(x)=1\chi_A(x) = 1χA(x)=1 if x∈Ax \in Ax∈A, and χA(x)=0\chi_A(x) = 0χA(x)=0 otherwise. It is used in probability theory, measure theory, and in computer science for bitwise operations and set membership testing in algorithms and databases.

131. What is De Morgan's Law and how is it applied in logic?
Answer: De Morgan's Laws are two transformation rules that relate conjunctions and disjunctions of logical statements through negation. The laws state:
¬(P∧Q)=¬P∨¬Q\neg (P \land Q) = \neg P \lor \neg Q¬(P∧Q)=¬P∨¬Q
¬(P∨Q)=¬P∧¬Q\neg (P \lor Q) = \neg P \land \neg Q¬(P∨Q)=¬P∧¬Q
These rules are fundamental in simplifying logical expressions, designing digital circuits, and converting logical formulas into normal forms.

132. Differentiate between a clique and an independent set in graph theory.
Answer: A clique in a graph is a subset of vertices such that every two distinct vertices are connected by an edge, forming a complete subgraph. An independent set, on the other hand, is a subset of vertices such that no two vertices in the set are adjacent. Cliques represent groups with mutual connections, while independent sets represent mutually exclusive entities. Both concepts are crucial in social network analysis, scheduling, and optimization problems.

133. What is the principle of duality in Boolean algebra?
Answer: The principle of duality in Boolean algebra states that every algebraic expression remains valid if the operators and identity elements are interchanged—specifically, replacing AND (·) with OR (+), OR with AND, 0 with 1, and 1 with 0. For example, the dual of A+0=AA + 0 = AA+0=A is A·1=AA \cdot 1 = AA·1=A. Duality helps verify Boolean expressions and simplifies logic design in computer systems.

134. Explain the concept of closure in set operations.
Answer: Closure is a property of a set under a specific operation where performing the operation on elements of the set always results in an element that is also in the set. For example, the set of integers is closed under addition because adding two integers always yields another integer. Closure is a critical property in algebraic structures like groups, rings, and monoids.

135. What is the difference between symmetric and antisymmetric relations?
Answer: A relation RRR on a set is **symmetric** if for every (a,b)∈R(a, b) \in R(a,b)∈R, the pair (b,a)∈R(b, a) \in R(b,a)∈R also holds. A relation is **antisymmetric** if for every (a,b)∈R(a, b) \in R(a,b)∈R and (b,a)∈R(b, a) \in R(b,a)∈R, then a=ba = ba=b. For example, "is a sibling of" is symmetric, while "less than or equal to" is antisymmetric. These concepts are central in relation theory, database design, and order theory.

© Author and Publisher 2024

9 789369 728657

Printed at Repro India Ltd.